MW01274511

INVITED TO SPEAK

TELL IT TRUE, MAKE IT VIVID, KEEP IT TIGHT

JOSEPH BEDNARIK

ACKNOWLEDGEMENTS

Gratitude to artist LORAN SCRUGGS for permission to use her artwork *Writers Heart* (2015) as the image on the front cover.

Thanks to PETER MULVEY for permission to quote the entirety of his song "The Dreams."

Deep appreciation to CLEMENS STARCK and his publisher, EMPTY BOWL, for permission to include five poems from *Cathedrals and Parking Lots: Collected Poems*.

All drawings are by JACOB BOLES
(except "Postcards from your Spiritual Journey").

Book designed by CONNER BOUCHARD-ROBERTS.

ISBN 979-8-9904537-0-8

OVER
under
PUBLISHING

This book is dedicated to

REV. BRUCE BODE

in appreciation for his
generous invitations

&

LIESL, OPAL, and LOUISE
dearest beloveds

CONTENTS

WARNING: CONTENT

At some point throughout these pages, may you encounter words, phrases, ideas, images, thoughts, memories, stories, quotes, and emotions that spark you to feel

amused confused pissed overjoyed disgusted annoyed
contemplative aware alert alive befuddled hungry awake

and, if all goes well, at some point may your heart burst into blossom and hummingbirds swoop near, curious about the bright new flower.

Thinking is fun.

Give energy.

Enunciate.

Tell true stories.

Make it vivid.

Keep it tight.

FOREWORD:
ADVICE ON A 3×5 CARD

"What *was* that?" a woman asked me after the service. "That didn't sound like a sermon."

Music to my ears!

I shy away from the word "sermon," though what I do on Sunday mornings looks very much like someone delivering a sermon.

"Let's call what that was a 'riprap,'" I replied.

I had accepted an invitation to speak to a small-town Unitarian Universalist congregation on Mother's Day morning. The presentation, "They Saw Two Heads," riffed on the birth story of my twin daughters to celebrate the fierce love of mothers, to howl at an ancient tragedy, and to try to bend the brutal bell curve that defines "normal" into an inclusive circle. I teared up while delivering the talk, which gave permission for others to tear up. (I frequently tear up while delivering a talk and have learned the hard way to never blow my nose while wearing a hot mic.)

"Riprap? Well, I *needed* that riprap this morning," the woman said, smiling.

That short exchange is exactly why I accept invitations to speak on Sunday mornings. For me, magic happens when seekers gather to co-create a space called sanctuary and collectively practice the art of paying attention.

When I first started delivering Sunday morning talks, a seasoned minister (and please note that I am not a minister) advised me that there are four people in attendance at every service, and that

I needed to consider each:

~ Someone is enjoying the best day of their life.

~ Someone is suffering the worst day of their life.

~ Someone is brand new to the congregation and feeling eager and buoyant.

~ Someone is sick and tired of the stupid place and can't wait to hit the exit.

To speak to each person and the group, I developed an aspirational goal: *Don't be boring*.

I also embraced the models and advice of four extraordinary people I have had the pleasure to meet, study, talk with, and befriend: professor Aryeh Kosman, actor Stephen Tobolowsky, poet Clemens Starck, and writer Jim Harrison.

Aryeh Kosman was a towering intellect and a legendary scholar of Aristotle and Plato, and he reminded all his students, "Thinking is fun." I love both fun and thinking, so I took every philosophy class I possibly could with Aryeh. I also began working for him as a handyman and landscaper and had the pleasure of cleaning out his attic and garage and inheriting his castoffs, including a vintage barber's chair. Our very first verbal exchange started with a generic get-to-know-you question.

"Is that your dog?" I asked.

Aryeh looked at the dog sleeping at his feet, then to me, and asked with a raised eyebrow, "Don't you think he's his own dog?"

Any reference I make to Socrates or Plato is, by extension, a reference to Aryeh. One pilgrimage on my travel itinerary is to visit

Aryeh's grave, where I will find this line from A.R. Ammons engraved into stone:

ANYTHING LOOKED AT CLOSELY BECOMES WONDERFUL.

Stephen Tobolowsky is an enthralling storyteller, and I am a devoted listener to and student of his podcast, *The Tobolowsky Files*. I listen carefully to each episode and marvel at how he draws me in, makes me care, makes me laugh and cry and think. I can *feel* the emotions in his voice—Tobo is a talented voice actor—and those emotions sound genuine. Tobo's grounding principle is easy to remember: "Tell true stories."

Clemens Starck is an older brother from a different set of parents. His poetry readings are legendary, and he considers the poem on the page to be sheet music, with the poem through his voice the song. He takes live performance very seriously and shared with me his wisdom about presenting in front of an audience: "Enunciate your words and give energy. If you're not giving energy, you're sucking energy," which I took to mean "Don't suck." One of my favorite talks, "Figure Out Something," was co-presented with Clem. He presented his poems and I talked about those poems. We performed this "dog and pony show" (Clem's words) several times, and the listeners those mornings responded with joyful enthusiasm and eagerness to buy Clem's books, especially the wonderfully titled collection *Cathedrals and Parking Lots*.

Jim Harrison. When I was twenty I took a leave of absence from college, put myself on a reading fast, and hitchhiked from east to west across the United States. My plan was to hitchhike around the world, though I only got as far as Kyoto. When I landed in Berkeley, California, I interviewed to become part of a communal house and was delighted to be admitted as the fourth and final member of the household. As I was getting to know my new housemates, I explained my reading fast, and my housemate

Michael—who had studied with Harold Bloom at Yale—handed me a beat-up paperback of Jim Harrison's first novel, *Wolf: A False Memoir.*

"When you're ready for breakfast, read this."

A month or so later I followed those instructions, broke my fast, and read the book. The effect was akin to the impact of reading Camus's novel *The Fall* or Thoreau's masterpiece *Walden. Wolf* was far more than a mere lightning strike—it was an entire weather system roaring in from the mountains. From that moment on, Jim's books—fiction, poetry, nonfiction—became touchstones and beacons in my idiosyncratic canon. His poetry is sacred text for me. As a publisher, I enjoyed the great good fortune of serving as Jim's poetry editor for nearly twenty years, though that job also came with breathing clouds of secondhand smoke. From Jim I borrowed the three words written on a card tacked above his writing desk: *Make it vivid.*

I also lodged in my heart a line of his poetry:

> God is terse. The earth's proper scripture could be carried on a three-by-five card.

All the guidance mentioned above could be carried on a 3×5 card, with room to spare.

~ Thinking is fun.

~ Give energy.

~ Enunciate.

~ Tell true stories.

~ Make it vivid.

~ Keep it tight.

While the seven ripraps presented in this slender book were originally presented to listening ears, they are now presented for reading eyes. It is my great hope that this sheet music can deliver the songs.

Our goal should be to live life in radical amazement . . . get up in the morning and look at the world in a way that takes nothing for granted. Everything is phenomenal; everything is incredible; never treat life casually. To be spiritual is to be amazed.

~ Rabbi Abraham Joshua Heschel

I long to accomplish a great and noble task,
but it is my chief duty to accomplish small tasks
as if they were great and noble.

~ Helen Keller

In twenty miles I ought to be able
to figure out something.

~ Clemens Starck

Omit needless words.

~ Strunk and White, *The Elements of Style*

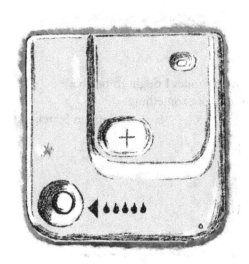

THEY SAW TWO HEADS

I BOW to all the children of mothers this morning.

Mother's Day is perhaps the most democratic of all our holidays, celebrated in many cultures throughout the world.

We all have mothers, and for the most part this sorority of women is nurturing, loving, fiercely loyal, and to a person want a safe and sane world for us, their children. And it makes sense that if *this* mother wants the best for her children, and *that* mother wants the best for her children—and since we're all children—then there is a rich opportunity for a common understanding that goes something like "Hey, here's a bright idea: let's create a world in which all mothers get to nurture and raise their children with the best that this glorious planet has to offer."

I have a deep resonance for Mother's Day because I became a father on Mother's Day. Twice, on the same day.

It was Mother's Day, and my wife, Liesl, and I had begun our perfectly planned Sunday. I was reading the book that I was doggedly trying to finish—a book I had tried to read many times but had always failed to complete. I recognize the irony of my reading choice with a pregnant woman lying beside me: Albert Camus's *The Plague*. I was just getting to some juicy existential part when Liesl cried out, "My water broke!"

We had planned a homebirth and were working with two very experienced midwives. They were the classic couple: one was a stout Earth Mother with a booming laugh and the other was a tall and willowy listener. They were very supportive of our desire to keep the pregnancy as low-tech as possible, to not bother with ultrasounds or tests like amniocentesis.

Keep in mind, this was Eugene, Oregon, in the 1990s, when you could burn sage on the night of a waxing moon and conjure your natural shamanic powers.

But amniocentesis is not shamanic. It's a profoundly scientific diagnostic test that can indicate whether a developing fetus will have a chromosome abnormality.

When Liesl and I discussed whether to get this diagnostic test, we asked ourselves what we would do if the result were positive, if the test indicated, for instance, that our child would have Down syndrome.

What. Would. We. Do?

We stared at each other in silence for a long minute. The silence grew, and in that silence, a body was growing inside another body—a body and brain and heart, conceived with great love and growing inside another body.

That body swelling Liesl's belly was our child, who would give shape and meaning to our lives forever, just as we had given shape to our parents' lives, and they to theirs, in a lineage that stretched back to *every* creation story.

Our silence, our unwillingness to answer the question with verbalized words, was as close to an amniocentesis as we got. We also never bothered with an ultrasound. It was always an option, but only if we felt it medically necessary. And we never felt it necessary.

You should also know this about the story: our midwives were also working with friends of ours, let's call them John and Ann, who were also having their first child. Like us, they were low-tech homebirthing types. They were a month or so ahead of us in their pregnancy, and we were all excited when Ann's water broke. Things were getting very real for *both* of these sets of first-time parents.

This was before the smartphone/social media era, so we kept in touch through a designated contact as hours turned into a day, and a day turned into most of another day.

Exhausted, Ann and John decided to finish labor at the hospital. And somewhere between their home and the hospital, the baby inside Ann died.

At the hospital, Ann gave natural birth to a beautiful boy, with ten fingers, ten toes. The nurses carefully washed and wrapped the baby and handed him to his father and mother—to meet, to hold, to fall in love, and to grieve.

They named their little guy, and later that year his ashes—ashes that could be cupped in a palm—were sprinkled into the Pacific Ocean.

Every time Ann looks at that vast ocean she thinks of her first child, a son, how her love is in that ocean. How her love *is* that ocean. This is a mother's love—*oceanic*—part of a ceaseless cycle of ocean to cloud to rain to river to ocean.

Birth to life to death—sometimes not in that order.

In their twenty years of serving the pregnant families of Eugene, our midwives had never lost a baby. That was the phrase they used, "lost a baby." And Liesl and I knew exactly where our baby was—alive and well and floating in an ocean of pure and clean and warm amniotic fluid. The womb. The first ocean-home for all of us. This family—*our* family—was their next client.

Liesl and I had a very sober meeting with the midwives and we decided to continue as planned. And then, on Mother's Day morning, water broke—the birthing of our child started in earnest. Adrenaline-addled father leaps out of bed, calls midwives, and begins moving furniture.

Midwives arrive, perform an exam, determine that the head isn't quite where it should be, and offer this option: go to the hospital for an ultrasound, then return home for labor and delivery.

Perfect!

True to our homebirthy roots, we didn't have an ob-gyn. We got the doc on call and she greased up Liesl's belly for the ultrasound. On the live feed to the monitor, the doctor pointed out the spine and the heart and the head of our baby.

It was an amazing sight to see.

Then Liesl made a request: "Would you scan this bump at the top of my belly?" And when the ultrasound wand went to the other side of Liesl's pregnant belly, a second human head appeared on the monitor. There were seven people in the hospital room and this was the sound, times seven:

Liesl burst into tears and I started laughing. Two natural reactions that made perfect sense.

There was so much confusion, so much change, so fast. At one point, stressed from the seemingly out-of-control transition from the most crunchy-granola ideals of a gently assisted birth in our own home to the institutional and surgical delivery by strangers, Liesl began crying.

She said she didn't know whether she had enough love for two babies.

Then one of our midwives put her face very close to Liesl's tearstained face and gave her a message—mother to mother: "Love doesn't work that way."

Love doesn't work that way.

This all happened on Mother's Day 1997, and I've told this story on many occasions. After all, surprise twins are rare in this day and age.

"It's a girl!"

Pause.

"It's another girl!"

It makes for a good tale.

We were prepared for only one child, so we needed to find more baby gear—*fast*. And that's when the white van pulled up. In one of the most heartrending scenes of my life, John and Ann, who had lost their baby the month before, brought us everything we needed.

Oceanic love.

Years later, when I was back in my hometown for a visit, my mother added to the story.

"Do you remember what you told me when you called me from the hospital? When you called me from the hospital about my very first grandchild?"

"No, Mom, I don't. What'd I say?"

"You said, 'They saw two heads,' and then you hung up!"

I cracked up, imagining my poor mother on the end of a three-thousand-mile phone line trying to envision her two-headed grandchild.

My poor mother. I would like to publicly apologize to her for this hideous gaffe.

Gaffe or no gaffe, I loved that line, "They saw two heads," so I worked it into the birth story. People loved that image: the accurate though completely misleading description of reality.

Then something happened that inspired me to reconsider.

I had occasion to tell our birth story and I included the usual "They saw two heads!" Like every other time I told the story, there was the burst of laughter. But after things settled down, a woman took me aside to share something privately. She was a mother, and looking me straight in the eyes she very earnestly said, "You know, there *are* two-headed people in the world." Then she let silence hang between us.

She was completely serious.

I nodded, ever so slightly, trying to express deep thoughtfulness on my face, though inside I was thinking, *Really? We're so PC, so squeaky clean, that I can't even call forth the image of two-headed people to help enliven a story?*

Nonetheless, I earnestly vowed to be more thoughtful, and true to my word, I stand before you now, on Mother's Day, to share the insights derived from "being more thoughtful":

Mother Love is the most divine and powerful force in the Universe. It is pervasive and deep and undeterred. This woman, this mother, was brave and insightful enough to defend, in the afterglow of a funny story, the rare and marvelous children born on the far edges of the human-body bell curve.

Most of us live most of the time our normal lives with "normal" bodies in the bulging normal middle. The weird is weird and, by definition, rare. Beautifully, extravagantly, marvelously rare. The teeming middle becomes the world, becomes normal, aka "the norm," and thus self-referentially beautiful and smart and right.

Emphasis here on *self-referentially* beautiful.

But you know, there *are* two-headed people in the world. And limbless people. Eyeless people. Intersex people. People with Down syndrome. The list could go and on, like the long tails of a bell curve.

These rare and marvelous people—to a person—all have mothers. And they live inside the warm heart of the founding principle of Unitarian Universalism: that every person has inherent worthiness and dignity.

Think about this for a moment. Every person has inherent worthiness and dignity. This principle does not blur the specific with the phrase "all people." This principle *sees* every person, as in you. And you. And you and you and you.

This is easy to say from within the comfortable middle of the bell curve, to people who look like "us."

The mother who pulled me aside and reminded me that there are two-headed people in the world was bravely stepping out of the bulging middle of the bell and defending the first UU principle at its farthest reaches, attempting something this world needs now more than ever. She was grabbing those long, pernicious ends of the bell curve—called exile and exclusion—and making them disappear by bending them together into a circle of inclusion.

A loving circle of inclusion.

This was one brave mother putting our religion into action, transforming a painful bell curve into a loving circle.

So let's turn back time and imagine that when I called my mother from the hospital the news was true, that they saw two heads— but only one body. Truth be told, I would have cried and cried. Liesl would have cried and cried. My mother would have cried and cried.

And then, after our crying, when our two-headed child was born, we would have fallen in love.

We would have fallen in love and become warriors and advocates and educators and activists from the far reaches of the bell curve, where we would be furiously forging circles. We would have raised our two-headed child—or, more accurately, our single-torsoed *children*—to be supple and courageous in the face of the relentless taunting and cruelty of the coarse and cutting bell curve.

But let's face it—that is fanciful conjecture. The real question is what to do moving forward, now that a mother reminded me—and by extension you—that there *are* two-headed people in the world. Truth be told, I still use that line—*They saw two heads!*—though after the laughter settles down, I've started adding another sentence to the story, a Mother Love empathy exercise to hopefully catalyze some thinking: "Have you ever imagined how wild and wonderful it would be to parent a two-headed child?"

AMEN.

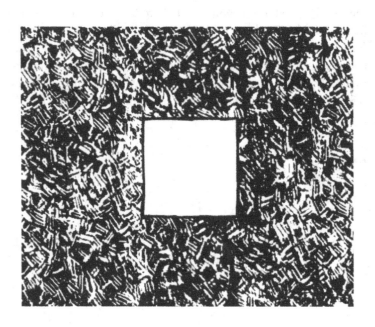

HOW QUIET SILENCE: [ ]

[Preceding this talk, pianist IKUE GOLDSTEIN performed John Cage's composition *4'33"* on a grand piano. "I've *always* wanted to play this piece for an audience," she exclaimed when she was asked to do so. Ikue's performance left the congregation speechless and awed.]

S ILENCE is

~ a concept

~ a destination

~ a metaphor

~ a challenge

~ a destiny

~ a political protest

~ oppression to fight against

~ a state of being to meditate toward

~ a religious experience

~ a claim to stake

~ when naturally occurring, something to preserve

~ the first right you are reminded of when arrested:
    You have the right to remain silent. Anything
    you say can and will be used against you.

[ ]

I have always been troubled by the phrase "can and will be used
against you," so this morning, together, inside this sacred space,
we claim that right and practice our first transformation: we can
and will say silence—and this silence will be used *for* us.

[ ]

All cultures and religions, art and poetry, music and relationships
make time and space for quiet and silence. Something *powerful* is
at work, and we humans build and pray and paint and sing and
strum and bow and love to call that silence deeper into ourselves.

[   ]

Ram Dass says, "The quieter you become, the more you can hear." The implication is both inner and outer hearing. I wonder how quiet one must become to be silent. To hear, we must listen. There are so many ways *not* to listen. Silence implies profound listening.

[   ]

The composition of this piece began in my family's living room, a welcoming space in a loving home with a large table, wood stove, piano, paintings, and books. At the exact moment I started writing, a loud, animated, and extended discussion about math homework—sines, cosines, tangents—began. I was forced to wear protective ear guards, normally used for those working with weed whackers and chain saws. These ear guards dampened the sounds of the voices and allowed me muffled quiet to concentrate on silence.

[   ]

When will that dog stop barking?

When will that baby stop crying?

When will that diesel engine stop idling?

When will that leaf blower run out of gas?

When will the neighbor turn off that hideous music?

Who on earth uses a circular saw at 7:30 in the morning?

[   ]

One of the most inspirational gifts I've ever received during my travels was bestowed in SeaTac airport, when I discovered a woman sitting in meditation, sitting in a full lotus position on the floor, sitting and meditating in a busy, bustling terminal. When I saw her I stopped and stood and watched her meditate for several long minutes. I also witnessed hundreds of travelers flow past to get to their gates, to get to their flights, to get to their cars, to get to their baggage.

Many glanced at the quiet, meditating woman as they hustled past.

The image that came to my mind was of a great solid still silent boulder in the middle of a swift river.

That silent boulder-woman comes to mind every time I walk into an airport. *I could become a boulder-woman,* I think, as I drag my baggage toward the gate.

[ ]

What kinds of silence make you uncomfortable? On radio interviews, silence—even thoughtful silence—is called "dead air," and it is not welcome. Keep talking . . . keep enlivening the air.

[ ]

Silence enlivens.

[ ]

My first religious experience of silence came when I attended Quaker services in college. We gathered in a historic meeting-house, where pews were aligned in concentric squares, with all pews facing inward toward a central focal point. We came into the meetinghouse without speaking and sat in a pew. We settled down.

We sat quietly together in a room where the highest purpose was to allow people to sit quietly together and listen for the Spirit. Sit quietly toward silence. If and when the Spirit of Christ moved someone to speak, that person would stand and give voice to language. Those words were considered by all who heard. After the person was done speaking, they would sit down and the quiet would settle once again. Perhaps after a while another person would be moved by the Spirit, stand, and speak.

We were being woven together by quiet, by silence, by necessary words given voice in real time.

At one of the finest Quaker services I ever attended, not a word was spoken. Not. One. Word. When the service was over, everyone rose, greeted each other, and remarked on how powerfully the silence spoke.

[   ]

Quakers understand the moral messages silence can send.

In the 1980s, when students and activists pressured Haverford College to divest from companies that were invested in apartheid South Africa, students lined the sidewalk leading to the building where a decisive board meeting was to take place. Everyone stood in silence. You could *feel* the silence, the meaning and resolve of the silence.

Each board member had to walk through a corridor of silent witnesses urging them to make the right, the moral, the just, the sound decision.

[   ]

For years, women dressed in black clothes have stood in silence in cities all over the world. They mourn the losses of war and advocate for peace.

The movement—called Women in Black—may have started in Israel, where Jewish and Arab women gathered to protest the violence of the Palestinian/Israeli conflict.

Women in Black may have begun in Central and South America, in recognition of those who "disappeared" during the years of political unrest.

There is every reason to believe that it started in both places simultaneously, then spread across the globe.

On Monday, like the hundreds of Mondays before this one, several women dressed in black stood silently on the sidewalk along Water Street in Port Townsend, Washington. One woman held a small black sign with white letters that read "PEACE."

As I approached these women I could feel the resolve of their silence, how their silence was the same as the silence of women in black clothes in Berlin and Boston and Beirut.

I nodded and accepted a leaflet—black letters standing together on white paper.

[   ]

In the early 1950s, composer John Cage visited an anechoic chamber at Harvard University.

An anechoic chamber is a room designed to be perfectly soundproof.

Cage expected that he would experience absolute silence. Rather, he became acutely aware of two droning noises, one high and one low. After Cage exited the chamber, he spoke with the engineer, who informed the composer that those drones were the sounds of his own body—he was hearing his nervous system, the high drone, and the circulation of his blood, the low drone. Of the experience, Cage said, "Until I die, there will be sounds."

[   ]

Friends and family with Buddhist leanings have traveled far and wide to attend silent retreats where they live, briefly, in community with like-minded students and practitioners. When they return to their so-called normal life, they tell stories of how profound it can be to not speak, how much effort it takes to try to quiet the mouth and quiet the mind—or more accurately, how much *non*-effort it takes to quiet the mind, how much *non*-effort it takes to cultivate attention and to approach, if not experience, silence as a spiritual state.

And they admit that even though words are not coming out of their mouths, the words themselves have not stopped. Just because the mouth is shut does not mean that the mind is quiet.

It is quite easy to physically stop speaking. That said, it can be an agonizing, pressurized challenge to not speak, to not speak, to not speak, to not speak . . . to be forced to listen to the ceaseless chattering in your mind; to hear the monkeys in your mind screaming, leaping from treetop to treetop; to try to tamp down the chatter, to quiet the monkeys; to avoid the chatter; to dance with the chatter; to ignore the chatter; how the chatter taunts and laughs and calls and snickers and smirks at your silence: *chatter chatter chatter chatter chatter chatter* . . .

One friend told me how, after three days of vegetarian meals and physically not talking, her chattering mind could take it no longer. She was sitting in meditation with many others—many, many others, all sitting quietly, all sitting toward silence. All of a sudden she could not help herself and she bellowed an astonishing word: *Sausages!*

Yes, she yelled *Sausages!* in a packed meditation hall.

The sizzling *s*'s that make up the word "sausages" vibrated one hundred sets of eardrums.

Some of those sitting in meditation let the event flow by, while other minds seized the sausages, the sizzling sausages—sausages on hot grills, in frying pans, pierced with sticks and cooked over coals on the beach with the chattering monkeys on a warm summer night. Sausages inside soft buns with mustard and ketchup, kosher dill pickles, and hot to the bite. Yes, thank you, I'd love a cold beer with my sausages and silence. *Pffft*.

[ ]

That high tone within you right now, that you cannot detect, is your nervous system.

That low tone that you cannot detect is your blood, circulating from your beating heart, oxygenating your body and brain.

You carry this music within you at all times.

[ ]

Religious scholars have yet to prove that the Buddha did not yell *Sausages!* while sitting silent in full lotus under the Bodhi tree.

[ ]

Composer John Cage's most famous piece of experimental music is entitled *4′33″*. It is a composition with three movements in which no musical sounds are made, no music is played.

The composition premiered in 1952, and imagine this: David Tudor, a young pianist, walks onto the stage, bows to polite applause, and sits at his instrument—a perfectly tuned grand piano.

He loosens his shoulders, stretches his neck a bit, adjusts the score open before him.

He then closes the lid and never touches the keys for the duration of the first movement.

36

He opens the keyboard lid, stretches again, then closes the lid at the beginning of the second movement. The third movement is similar to the previous two. When the piece concludes, the pianist rises from the bench, triumphant, bows, and walks offstage.

In his book *The Rest Is Noise,* classical music critic Alex Ross writes of this performance, "The music was the sound of the surrounding space. It was at once a head-spinning philosophical statement and a Zen-like ritual of contemplation. It was a piece that anyone could have written, as skeptics never failed to point out, but, as John Cage seldom failed to respond, no one else did."

[   ]

We are all invited to sit quietly with our instruments and listen to "the sound of the surrounding space" with great attention. High tone. Low tone.

[   ]

The title of Cage's composition, *4′33″*, indicates four minutes thirty-three seconds. In thinking and writing about this piece of experimental music, critics have noted that four minutes thirty-three seconds contains 273 seconds.

The number 273 is significant in that *minus* 273 degrees Celsius is a state called absolute zero, the lowest temperature possible, the temperature at which molecular motion ceases. Scientists have gotten close to but have never reached absolute zero; humans have also never reached absolute silence.

[   ]

How quiet silence?

[   ]

The Buddha played *4′33″* countless times—more than two thousand years before John Cage wrote the score.

[   ]

To riff on René Descartes's famous phrase "Cogito ergo sum" (I think therefore I am): I imagine *4′33″* at absolute zero ergo I hear silence.

[   ]

The perfect performance of *4′33″* takes place in an anechoic music hall at absolute zero.

[   ]

Lest we forget, *4′33″* is about music and sound, high and low tones, about being together in the sacred space of a music hall or sanctuary with a perfectly tuned instrument and a talented musician.

It is about listening.

It is, at its essence, about being alive, together, attentive. It is a great blessing to be together in intentional quiet, listening—as any Quaker or Buddhist might tell you.

[   ]

Terry Tempest Williams is a writer I deeply admire. She was born and raised in Utah and grew up in Mormon culture. From the time she was a little girl she loved words and stories and writing and the magic of books. Two key aspects of Mormon culture, for women, are to have children and to keep a journal. Terry's mother dutifully did both, and as the years passed the number of journals on her bookshelf—a bookshelf in a secret closet—grew.

The journals were deeply private, and Terry didn't even know her mother kept a journal. Year after year, journal after journal, a woman's daily life, deepest thoughts, and private dreams, recorded.

Like many who lived in Utah during the Cold War, Terry's mother was a "downwinder," and her body was exposed to radiation from aboveground nuclear testing. Terry's mother, like thousands in Utah, became sick with cancer. A week before she died, at age fifty-four, she told Terry—her writer-daughter who loved words and books and stories—that she could have her journals.

Weeks passed before Terry had the emotional strength to open the journals, to open her inheritance. She writes about the experience, "I finally sought out the journals as a lifeline that could pull me to solid ground."

> It was a beautiful winter day. Salt Lake City was a mirror of white light reflecting off recent snow. . . . Mother had left me her journals. It was my birthright to read them. . . . Now was the time.
>
> I opened the closet and pulled out the first journal. It was blank. I flipped through the empty pages. Nothing. I opened the second journal. It, too, was blank. As were the third journal, the fourth, the fifth, the sixth. I went through every journal on every shelf praying to find her script, but all I found was a collection of white pages perfectly bound. My mother had left me her journals, and all her journals were blank. I had hoped to find her deepest thoughts, her dreams, her struggles, alongside her wisdom. What she left me were her silences.

[   ]

I attended a reading at the Seattle Central Library where Williams read from her book *When Women Were Birds*, about the experience of her mother's journals.

It was a standing room–only crowd.

After her reading, she stepped from behind the lectern for the scheduled Q&A portion of the evening. Everyone sat in silence, processing the meanings of those blank journals and the subsequent thinking and writing and feeling and meditation expressed by the writer-daughter inheritor of those journals.

Silence filled the room and it felt just fine.

[   ]

I had another religious experience of encountered silence at the United Nations building in New York City. Inside that building I discovered a miraculous place, the Meditation Room, a small room with benches, an abstract mural, and a six-ton block of iron ore lit from above by a slender spotlight.

I was stunned.

In a city of eight million people, I was alone in this glorious room. Alone inside a room called the Meditation Room, inside a building called the United Nations.

I sat and watched the iron ore and thought of the meditating boulder-woman at SeaTac. I watched the light on top of the iron, then stood and approached the iron and held my hand above its surface so that my hand was lit by the spotlight and its shadow was cast onto the black surface: the weightless shadow of a hand atop six tons of iron ore.

I stood alone and speechless.

Upon exiting I wondered where the line of pilgrims was, a line stretching the length of Manhattan to experience that quiet with six tons of black iron and a slender beam of light.

[   ]

The philosopher Ludwig Wittgenstein concludes his revolutionary classic *Tractatus Logico-Philosophicus* with these words: "What we cannot speak about we must consign to silence."

[   ]

Dag Hammarskjöld, the second secretary-general of the United Nations, who designed the Meditation Room, wrote, "We all have within us a center of stillness surrounded by silence. This house [the United Nations], dedicated to work and debate in the service of peace, should have one room dedicated to silence in the outward sense and stillness in the inner sense."

[   ]

Poet Anna Swir [Świrszczyńska] served as a nurse during the 1944 Warsaw Uprising in World War II. She was captured by Nazis and was within thirty minutes of being executed. Fortunately, her life was spared, and with that life she wrote:

There Is a Light in Me

Whether in daytime or in nighttime
I always carry inside
a light.
In the middle of noise and turmoil
I carry silence.
Always
I carry light and silence.

[   ]

Poet Audre Lorde reminds everyone, "Your silence will not protect you."

[   ]

As the crow flies, the quietest place in the United States is within sixty miles of my home. In the Olympic National Park, within the Hoh Rain Forest, is a mossy patch called One Square Inch of Silence.

There is an organization to preserve this special place. According to their website:

> One Square Inch of Silence was designated on Earth Day 2005 to protect and manage the natural soundscape in the Olympic Park's backcountry wilderness. The logic is simple: if a loud noise, such as the passing of an aircraft, can impact many square miles, then a natural place, if maintained in a 100% noise-free condition, will also impact many square miles around it. It is predicted that protecting a single square inch of land from noise pollution will benefit large areas of the park.

Hear this radical equation: one square inch of mossy silence in a wilderness area on the Olympic Peninsula equals six tons of black-iron silence inside a skyscraper in Manhattan.

[   ]   [   ]   [   ]

Silence in the outward sense and stillness in the inner sense;

Women in Black the world over;

musicians playing *4′33″*;

blank journals;

anechoic chambers;

Quakers in wooden pews;

neighbors attending silent retreats;

boulder-woman sitting in full lotus in airports;

a six-ton slab of black iron;

One Square Inch of moss within a rain forest.

We inside this sanctuary:

[   ]   [   ]   [   ]

[AMEN.]

Clemens Starck

Cathedrals & Parking Lots

Collected
Poems

FIGURE OUT SOMETHING

Presented with poet Clemens Starck

[CLEMENS STARCK began this presentation by reading two of his poems, "Slab on Grade" and "Commuting."]

Slab on Grade

At dawn the concrete trucks
are already there: revving their engines,
rumbling and throbbing, one by one
maneuvering into position.
Enormous insects,
on command
they ooze from their huge revolving abdomens
a thick gray slime.

Insects attending to insects,
the crew fusses over them, nursing wet concrete
into the forms.

Someone to handle the chute,
a couple laborers mucking, one pulling mesh, and two
finishers working the screed rod—
this is called pouring
slab on grade.

What could be flatter or more nondescript
than a concrete slab?
For years people will walk on it,
hardly considering that it was put there
on purpose,
on a Thursday in August
by men on their knees.

Commuting

Firs on the hillside:
mist drifts through them like smoke.
White mist, black trees . . .
Headlights sweep the wet pavement.
Waiting at home
my son—he's ten, he wants to know
what we're here for.
Black firs. White mist.
Loose tools rattle in the back of the truck.
In twenty miles I ought to be able
to figure out something.

W HAT could be flatter or more nondescript
than a concrete slab?
For years people will walk on it,
hardly considering that it was put there
on purpose,
on a Thursday in August
by men on their knees.

I invite you to do an awareness exercise. Walk or roll into the Fellowship Hall and consider for a thoughtful minute what you are standing or sitting on.

Feel what you're being supported by.

It feels solid. It feels present. It has gravity.

That "it" is called "slab on grade."

A rectangle of nondescript concrete, put there on purpose, to support the building within which we would live and catalyze the principles of this liberal religion, this creedless religion, this religion that encourages everyone to listen carefully, think for themselves, and feel into the world . . . and then to listen and think and feel ever deeper.

And while we are listening and thinking and feeling, we often forget the slabs on grade of the world, and the work—and workers—required to make them a reality. This is not a criticism, simply an observation. Often it takes a poet to bring us back to essential things, to the fundamental building blocks of human culture. In this case, work. Foundational work. Work that brings us to our knees.

To be able to see slab on grade—to be able to perceive the necessary infrastructure upon which our lives are built—is a special sort of insight. And it is that insight that was a lightning bolt when, in my twenties, I attended a poetry reading in Eugene, Oregon, and my life quite literally changed.

Reading that night were two poets—one was a friend of a colleague, which was the reason I was in attendance, and then there was another poet, some carpenter from rural Oregon named Clemens Starck, of all things.

Thinking back on that poetry reading, I'm embarrassed to say that I've forgotten who the friend of the colleague was, though I have never forgotten Clemens Starck. That night he read the poem "Slab on Grade," and since that moment, I have never seen a concrete slab in quite the same way.

From that moment on, I saw those slabs connected to human work and intention, to purpose, to people actually doing the hard labor of making that slab possible—the slab that is a pure investment in creative possibility. Like a blank piece of paper, a hunk of wet clay, or a block of uncarved wood.

After that night in Eugene, a weird set of cosmic circumstances was put into motion that led me to my first job in publishing at a literary press where Clem—at age fifty-eight—was destined to publish his first book. That publishing house died years ago, though many of the books it produced are still circulating throughout the reader ecosystem. Every time I see one in a used bookstore, I give a little bow in honor of resilience.

The two poems that Clem read for us this morning—"Slab on Grade" and "Commuting"—are hard-won poems, and they live within one of those books from that long-gone publishing house, a book that continues to travel far and wide: *Journeyman's Wages.*

Clem and I worked closely together on that book, and in the course of so doing, became friends. We also celebrated the success of that book, as it won several important literary awards and received abundant review attention, not only because it is a deeply insightful book about working and living in the world but also because it was the debut of an unknown writer who was closing in on sixty.

For those late bloomers in the room, hope springs eternal!

Clem has lived a fascinating life of hard work, deep reading, and world travel, and for reasons that I encourage you to discover in his book *Studying Russian on Company Time*, he was in the collapsed Soviet Union when *Journeyman's Wages* won a coveted booksellers award. Since Clem was out of the country, I served as his stand-in at the awards ceremony. When his name was called, I approached the lectern and accepted the award on his behalf. And looking out at hundreds of booksellers—people whose livelihood is connecting books to readers—I read "Commuting." It was the first poem I ever presented in public. When I read the final lines—"In twenty miles I ought to be able / to figure out something"—I heard soft inhalations of breath.

I have never forgotten the sound of that communal breath. It was, for me, a holy sound. The sound of what a good poem—coupled with genuine attention—can do. Of what a good poem can accomplish when people listen. It is the sound of all of us thinking and feeling and breathing, alone together in the universe, trying to figure out what this gift of a warm beating heart actually is.

We have all been there. Alone in a vehicle. Driving at night. Pretending we are in control. Looking out at the slender patch of road illuminated by our headlights. And thinking. *Hard.*

In the decades since *Journeyman's Wages* won that award, Clem and I have become dear friends. Clem is a full quarter-century older than me, so he serves as one of those elders I look to, to see how they navigate and negotiate the world. When I told him, more than twenty years ago, that my wife was pregnant, I remember that his face brightened into a huge smile and he just laughed and laughed his congratulations. He smiled so wide I could see his gold dental work glinting in the sunlight. Clearly he knew something about the parental journey I was about to embark upon, because he was many years down that particular road. Though, truth be told, it did not comfort me that one of his poems has a line that refers to "the savagery of family life." I have repeated that phrase—"the savagery of family life"—thousands of time since my twin daughters were born. Not that my daughters are savages—or that I became one—but sometimes the daily, weekly, hourly grind of family life can ignite our savage, primitive brain.

And that savagery may be the precise reason why his poem "Commuting" is one of the poems I have committed to memory, with the provocative lines

> Waiting at home
> my son—he's ten, he wants to know
> what we're here for.

For me that line goes to the vibrant core of Unitarian Universalism: the free and responsible search for truth and meaning. There is nothing more free and responsible—and pure—than a young child asking their parent—their elder—the hardest, largest questions, like "What are we here for?"

Sit with that for a tender moment and think of your own ten-year-old self holding your beloved dead cat or your dead dog and looking up to an elder for the reason why. Tears streaming down cheeks with the realization that life has turned to death and death means gone. Misha is gone. It is *the* existential question that has confronted every person who has ever lived, and we look to others—through gifts like family, friendship, art, and religion—to help us puzzle through the question.

And is there anything more humbling than the scene of a person commuting home alone from work in the dark and thinking to themselves, "In twenty miles I ought to be able to figure out something"?

The bone-tired worker commuting home in clothes splattered with concrete from the slab she helped pour that Thursday.

> In twenty miles I ought to be able
> to figure out something.

I love that the poem does not reach for an answer, or *the* answer, only "to figure out something."

We are all trying to figure out something.

As such, I have taken the poem "Commuting" into my life as a sacred text—a gorgeous poem that does honor to the children who ask universal questions and the work-weary mortals who live into their deepest moments, trying to respond.

The parent commuting home for dinner and a shower, who enjoys hearing that *pffffts* of a beer opening and a smoke on the porch, then helps with math homework and dishes and reads the kids some fairy tales from the thick Grimm's anthology with the broken binding.

After the story, and lights out, silence settles in the dark room. The father listens to the son breathe those breaths that approach the borderland of crying.

"Papa?"

"Yes?"

"Why did Misha have to die?"

The papa closes his eyes in the dark and can't help but see the concrete truck oozing gray slime from its revolving abdomen. The papa hears the tools rattling in the back of his truck. The papa feels the ache of his muscles, especially his lower back and knees, the touch of arthritis in the elbow of his hammer arm. Today's commute arrived right here, right now, loving parent to questioning child, fellow traveler to fellow traveler.

The man takes a breath and begins to speak in something like a whisper . . .

[Clem presents the next poem.]

Why Buddhists Don't Kill Flies

By actual count there are twenty-eight flies
stuck to the flypaper
dangling from a beam in the kitchen,
twenty-eight sentient beings.

Recorded live
in an auditorium far from the Himalayas,
the Gyuto monks—a Tantric choir—are chanting,
making unearthly sounds.

My wife and I are at the table
drinking coffee, listening. Our daughter's perfume
floats down the stairs,
impinging on us.

This table measures three-and-a-half foot by six.
On it are books and flowers, a basket
of tangerines. If you ask, I will say
we are happy.

And if you ask why Buddhists don't kill flies . . .
Figure it yourself!
Exiled monks. Twenty-eight flies.
A kitchen in Oregon. A mountain in Tibet.

By quote-unquote actual count, twenty-eight dead flies are the opening image. What an extraordinarily grotesque way to begin a poem: a strip of flypaper dangling from a kitchen beam and dotted with dozens of corpses—dead sentient beings. Unstated in the poem are the twenty-ninth and thirtieth flies circling the strip of flypaper, buzzing toward the trap that will end their lives. How utterly violent and cruel within a kitchen otherwise filled with such life-affirming abundance.

My guess is that ninety-nine percent of those here inside this sanctuary are not the person put forward in the expression "She wouldn't harm a fly." Consider: the lowly fly as the inspiration for philosophical and religious consideration. The lowly fly with its miraculous eyes and superpower abilities to fly and defy gravity by walking on walls and ceilings.

I stand before you as a person who has willfully killed thousands of miraculous flies—even vacuumed them out of the air using a shop vac—to consider again the words of poet Marge Piercy that we read aloud when lighting the chalice: "Life is the first gift, love is the second, and understanding the third."

Life is the first gift. And when we act with design to take that gift from another sentient being—be that being a mosquito, fly, cockroach, mouse, rat, chicken, deer, salmon—we are making a choice to render violence that other devout believers would not make for deeply considered religious reasons.

Why is this?

Why do millions of other human beings living on this planet make a distinctly different choice for perfectly sound religious reasons? This is the question driving the poem. From the dead flies stuck to the dangling strip of flypaper, the poem pulls back to consider other sentient beings in this domestic scene—a husband and a wife—with their senses fully engaged: tasting coffee, smelling perfume, seeing the visual delight of flowers and tangerines, hearing the sound of monks chanting. The poet says, "If you ask, I will say / we are happy."

Happy because, it seems to me, the table—which is as flat and rectangular as the concrete slab poured last Thursday—holds upon it many treasures of culture that are within easy reach: cups of coffee, a basket of fruit, a vase of flowers, a stack of books.

Happy because the poet is sitting at the table with two gifts: life and love.

And happy in the face of the world's complications and pain, namely death and exile. Think of the potent word combination "exiled monks." Years ago, I had the good fortune of seeing and hearing Gyuto monks live in concert, and the hair on my neck is still standing up from that experience.

In this complicated world, there are very few answers as easy and straightforward as "This table measures three-and-a-half foot by six" or "By actual count there are twenty-eight flies." And take special note that the poet does not come right out and say that he is happy; rather, he is responding to a theoretical question, "if you ask." If you don't ask, he is simply within his life, engaging his senses, defending his food against flies, and listening intently with his wife to exiled monks chant "unearthly sounds" in a language the poet does not understand.

Happy, here, home. And then the second question arises:

> And if you ask why Buddhists don't kill flies . . .
> Figure it yourself!

Again, back to the words of our chalice lighting, "Life is the first gift, love is the second, and understanding the third."

"Figure it yourself" is the signpost toward the third gift: understanding. Nobody on earth can hand you understanding. You, truly, have to figure it yourself, and getting that third gift can be real work. It can be work that brings you to your knees. Certainly, others can help—poets, for instance.

And consider that word "figure," which appears at the close of both the poems "Commuting" and "Why Buddhists Don't Kill Flies."

> In twenty miles I ought to be able
> to figure out something.

> And if you ask why Buddhists don't kill flies . . .
> Figure it yourself!

And to "figure"—to work toward the third gift of understanding—is the free and responsible search for truth and meaning. To figure is the core activity of our liberal religious tradition.

So the invitation is this: during your commute home from church, try to "figure out something." You may or may not realize an insight. Regardless, when you get home, you can at least find a tape measure and figure the dimensions of your table. On the table, you could place a basket of fruit, some books and flowers—perhaps snowdrops floating on clear water. You could sit at the table and read a poem or listen to music. And then, when a miraculous sentient being lands on the table, ask yourself, *Why is it that Buddhists don't kill flies?*

And what I figure to do now is let our special guest have the final word, with two poems.

Regarding the Eclipse

Chances are I'll never tell
the story of how I found myself
adrift at sea
in a twelve-foot dinghy with a single oar;
or how, once, in the mountains
called Sierra Nevada,
trapped on a snowbound freight train,
my intrepid companions and I
existed for several days
on a fifty-pound sack of frozen marshmallows.

In retrospect
you could call it adventure, but at the time
it was nothing special. Anyway,
some events—like cloud formations
or teenage children—
are completely inexplicable.

My ambitions were nebulous at best.
All I ever wanted to be was a glassblower
or a wood carver
or failing that, a utility infielder.
A career in the Foreign Service
looked promising once, but I couldn't feature myself
in formal attire
on a balcony overlooking the capital . . .

What would I be doing there?
Serving cocktails
to the Peruvian attaché's voluptuous wife?

And so it is that I stand
on the sagging porch of a tumbledown house
regarding the lunar eclipse
through binoculars held steady by my stalwart left hand.
With the other I gesticulate wildly,
but fail to observe
any change
in the shadow cast by this earth on the moon.

Misha

Under the house is where I found him
huddled, barely alive,
a bundle of soft white fur
emitting one last feeble *miaow* as I crawled toward him.
This is how Misha died. My cat. My little pal.

Nine lives, they say. And so I thought
by stroking him and talking to him, murmuring his name
over and over again,
maybe I could love him
back to life.
It didn't work. This must have been his ninth.

While he lay dying on the hearth beside the woodstove
next to me, I finally
dozed off . . .
and dreamt that he had come alive,
miraculously leaping up and scampering around the room.

My son was with me in the dream,
and together we tried stopping him, afraid
he might harm himself
or disappear.

But then, without speaking, we both realized
he had already left his body.
This was his spirit passing through, on its way out
the open window.

It's good to have a cat. Even better
to have a son.

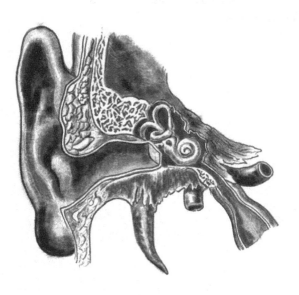

Non-uments and Toppled Statues

I STAND before you as a human being who can be profoundly affected by monuments.

I have gone out of my way to visit monuments, to be in their presence and witness them in body and spirit and was even planning a Southern road trip to go visit a monument when our global pandemic postponed that journey for another time.

Note the provisional "postponed," rather than the permanent "canceled," because hope springs eternal.

I remember visiting the Vietnam Memorial in Washington, DC, and being swallowed by the gravity of the black marble, being overwhelmed by the names engraved in black marble, and tracing my trigger finger along the letters that spelled the name of a man I never knew . . . and feeling tears rise.

I remember visiting the 9/11 Memorial in New York and being swallowed by the massive holes in the earth, being overwhelmed by the sheets of water falling along the smooth stone and down,

down, ever down into darkness. I remember silently tracing the tip of my index finger along the engraved letters that spelled the name of a pregnant woman I never knew . . . and feeling tears rise. We knew she was pregnant because the engraving "and her unborn child" told us so.

I remember my first trip to below the Mason–Dixon line, in the 1980s, sitting my Yankee butt in a Greyhound bus in Philadelphia, the birthplace of this nation, and rolling south through the Carolinas, into Georgia, and on to the panhandle of Florida, stopping in cities and towns along the way and being stunned by the statues celebrating the Confederacy and the glorious cause of the Civil War, by seeing Confederate flags flutter in bright sunshine atop tall poles in front of government buildings. No tears rose on those occasions, only disbelief.

I remember seeing the bright graffiti on the west side of the Berlin Wall, then walking through Checkpoint Charlie and being sobered by the ominous and fortified no-man's-land on the east side. The dark silhouette of an armed guard in a tower. Years later a friend sent me a chunk of the fallen wall, and I keep it as a tiny personal monument to the possibility of seismic political change.

I remember seeing massive statues of V. I. Lenin when I visited his namesake city—Leningrad—and then years later, after the collapse of the Soviet Union, seeing a similar statue in the Fremont neighborhood in Seattle. That powerful bronze statue had been found in a scrapyard in the Czech Republic, bought by an American, and shipped to Seattle for ironic display.

I remember screaming in a frothing rage at the radio when I heard an NPR story about Islamic fundamentalists blowing up the ancient and sacred Buddhas of Bamiyan because the monumental statues, which were carved into sandstone cliffs over one thousand years ago, were idols, and God does not abide by idols.

Tears.

Solemnity.

Silence.

Disbelief.

Irony.

Rage.

All these human responses in relation to monuments. And each of those vignettes prefaced with the words "I remember."

Monuments, as massive pieces of art and sculpture—whether political or religious or secular—are in service to memory and history. They also can confront our present and force us to ask *which* history; they can confront our present and force us to ask who we are, right now, and what history we are making in this—*our*—moment.

These monuments and statues can become fluid time travelers to past, present, and future . . . and back again, their presence asking, *Who are you?* And as in the case of V. I. Lenin, the intellectual godfather and leader of the Bolshevik revolution, a monument bearing his likeness can be toppled and then dragged to a scrapyard by new revolutionaries. The statue can be bought for the price of the metal, shipped across an ocean, then freighted across a continent, light years from its original context, and be re-erected in one of the richest cities in the world, home to multinational profit-driven corporations like Amazon and Microsoft and Boeing. A visitor is free to wonder, *Why is V. I. Lenin, the ur-Communist, here in Fremont near a burger joint?*

And there is an answer to that question, perhaps dozens of answers to that question.

As poet and novelist Jim Harrison wrote, "The answer is always in the entire story, not a piece of it." I love that quote and I think of it often in this complicated world that frequently strains for neat and tidy explanations. *The answer is always in the entire story, not a piece of it.*

Which says, in no uncertain terms, if you want the answer, then you need to listen to—and hear—the entire story. Not only that, but you must try to understand the story. And the entire story is almost always a mosaic of stories, each with varying complexities and layers of meaning—nuanced, shaded, with many facets and moods, from multiple and sometimes conflicting points of view.

The "answer"—if that is what you are actually looking for—can be hard to get at; the "answer" can shape-shift and shimmy, approach and recede; parts of the story may be hidden from view, whether by accident or intention.

Or we think we have the answer, build a monument to last one thousand years, settle in, and then the story expands or deepens with new information, with new discoveries, prompting the addition of a new piece to the mosaic. Or perhaps another whole mosaic being added to the original mosaic.

The pursuit of the entire story is inspired by the fourth principle of Unitarian Universalism: "The free and responsible search for truth and meaning."

We could—and perhaps should—call our fourth principle the Entire Story principle.

One example of the Entire Story principle that is deeply relevant to Unitarian Universalist history—especially as our denomination struggles with the white supremacy embedded in the culture broadly and in our denomination specifically—is the DNA test that proved beyond a shadow of a doubt that many Black Americans are the direct descendants of Thomas Jefferson.

Here is genetic science cutting through all the long-standing political debates, familial factions, historical hypothesis, arguments, counterarguments, half-truths, and outright lies.

Thomas Jefferson, a beloved Founding Father and Unitarian icon, wrote the immortal words in the Declaration of Independence "all men are created equal" while—at the exact same time the ink was drying on those legendary words—he owned human beings whom he enslaved.

Let us, for a moment, marvel that the phrase "all men are created equal" was written by an enslaver of men, as well as an enslaver of women and children, and let us place this fact as Exhibit A in the Museum of Cognitive Dissonance and Negative Capability.

And while the ink was drying on the phrase, a little girl named Sally Hemings, who was enslaved by Thomas Jefferson, was living at Jefferson's estate at Monticello. Two decades later, she would begin bearing Thomas Jefferson's children. Likely six children, all told. Three of them while Jefferson was serving as president of the United States.

With these Black children in mind, there is a warm and fuzzy story that the sexual relationship between Jefferson and Hemings was founded on love and respect. Yet, given the profound power differential between the two, it is more honest and rigorous to be *extremely* suspect of a loving relationship.

Until proven otherwise, any magical thinking that envisions Hemings as a willing and loving mistress is just that, magical thinking. Likely on the part of white people. To wit: Sally

Hemings's children—each and every one—were enslaved by their father the moment they were conceived and were only freed upon the execution of his will after he died.

It is notable that Jefferson, who enslaved more than six hundred people during his lifetime, freed only seven enslaved people total. No other enslaved person was ever granted their freedom, and the 130 enslaved people who belonged to the Jefferson estate at the time of his death were sold to help pay off debts. To sharpen this point, and perhaps to assuage our guilt, the selling of those human beings can be framed and contextualized as simply doing business during a specific era, a necessary and perfectly legal sacrifice on the blessèd altar of our most profound, sacred, fierce, and brutal religion, capitalism.

While those enslaved human beings were being exchanged for dollars and those human beings were carted away and disbursed throughout the South, where slavery continued to be legal, abolitionists in the North were circulating the dead president's words on antislavery to help finally bring an end to the evil.

Let us make this Exhibit B in our Museum of Cognitive Dissonance and Negative Capability. Jefferson's strong antislavery words are carved into his glorious memorial in Washington, DC. Imagine each letter painstakingly chiseled deep into white stone so they will never leave us, never be forgotten, will be forever memorialized, letter after letter, these words that passionately rage against slavery:

I TREMBLE FOR MY COUNTRY WHEN I REFLECT THAT GOD IS JUST, THAT HIS JUSTICE CANNOT SLEEP FOREVER. COMMERCE BETWEEN MASTER AND SLAVE IS DESPOTISM. NOTHING IS MORE CERTAINLY WRITTEN IN THE BOOK OF FATE THAN THAT THESE PEOPLE ARE TO BE FREE.

My guess is that over the decades, hundreds of thousands of Unitarians and Universalists have been in the presence of those chiseled words and felt a swelling pride that one of the icons of our religion wrote so eloquently against slavery.

So as we allow those words to work their magic on our minds and in our hearts, as we experience the awe and majesty of the classical architecture of the Jefferson Memorial, his erect and looming statuary presence, let us also do honor to the fourth principle, the Entire Story principle, with this realization: those antislavery words carved into the Jefferson Memorial are misleading for at least two reasons.

The first reason is that the concluding sentence, with those definitive words "these people are to be free," were lifted from Jefferson's autobiography and inserted as if they were the conclusion of a complete thought.

The second reason this memorial quote is misleading is that it is a classic case of lifting words out of context. Following the words "these people are to be free" are two more sentences, willfully ignored and not carved in white stone: "Nor is it any less certain that the two races, equally free, cannot live in the same government. Nature, habit, opinion has drawn indelible lines of distinction between them."

These words from a man who fathered children with a woman who was half Black, half white, the unacknowledged half sister of Jefferson's first wife, and who was enslaved by him. And imagine the enslaved mother, nursing the enslaved newborn, and the enslaver standing at the foot of the bed, gazing down on his legal property. If so desired, he could speculate on how much that little boychild would fetch on the open market once he came of age. Until then, nothing but maintenance costs of food, clothing, and shelter. Hard words to hear, though a scene painfully easy to imagine.

Perhaps, while looking at the miracle of human birth, while gazing at the inherent worthiness and dignity of his newest enslaved son or daughter—a relation Jefferson would never admit to publicly—perhaps he was composing in his brilliant and crystalline mind the beginnings of an idea that would also eventually be carved into stone at the Jefferson Memorial:

> I AM NOT AN ADVOCATE FOR FREQUENT CHANGES IN LAWS AND CONSTITUTIONS, BUT LAWS AND INSTITUTIONS MUST GO HAND IN HAND WITH THE PROGRESS OF THE HUMAN MIND. AS THAT BECOMES MORE DEVELOPED, MORE ENLIGHTENED, AS NEW DISCOVERIES ARE MADE, NEW TRUTHS DISCOVERED AND MANNERS AND OPINIONS CHANGE, WITH THE CHANGE OF CIRCUMSTANCES, INSTITUTIONS MUST ADVANCE ALSO TO KEEP PACE WITH THE TIMES.

Prescient words for 2020, the year of our pandemic, the year of our most recent economic collapse, the year of bitterly divided election politics, and the year of sustained and powerful protests for racial justice through changing the embedded systems that support white supremacy. To state the issue as plain as day: people are very pissed off and hurting, and rightfully so. They are tired of waiting for action.

In the two months since the murder of George Floyd, protesters have taken to the streets, to city council chambers, to statehouses, and to the nation's capital. Nearly one hundred memorial statues in twenty-one states—each and all honoring the Confederacy—have been removed or slated for removal. Ten of those memorial statues were toppled by protesters, including one in Seattle.

Imagine five or six ropes tied to a massive statue and a roiling crowd of protesters pulling with all their might, muscles straining. Imagine the statue not budging, and the crowd pulling ever harder, the ropes straining between the two opposing tensions. Slowly the giant stone or metal man begins to tip, until gravity takes over and finishes the job with a resounding crash. The crowd roars its approval and feels a surge of accomplishment, of history in the making.

When you look at the vacant pedestal, what do you see?

What. Do. You. See?

That fresh emptiness is a personal and communal Rorschach test.

Do you see progress? Chaos? Justice? Chaotic progress toward justice?

One possibility is that this empty pedestal has become a monument to space, reminding us that what we need to create is more space—for the multitude of voices and diversity of viewpoints—to create the necessary and loving space to allow the stories that make up the Entire Story to be seen, to be heard, to be honored, to be understood.

"The answer is always in the entire story, not a piece of it," writes the poet.

And if the world insists on placing something on those one hundred empty pedestals, I propose massive statues depicting the stapedius.

Stapedius!

The name sounds fitting for a mythical power, an entity *worthy* of a monument.

The stapedius is the smallest skeletal muscle in the human body, a muscle that is essential to the heavy lifting of listening.

The stapedius is about a millimeter long and located in the inner ear. Imagine a massive statue of the smallest human muscle, which would inspire listening, ever deeper, ever closer. We could be present in body at the once empty pedestal and gaze up at the extraordinary stapedius and realize that we have two of those small muscles, inside us, on either side of our brain. These monuments to the stapedius honor the fact that the smallest muscle in the human body is one of the strongest and most necessary, especially for our purposes at this moment. Now—today—this Sunday—let's create more space by listening for and telling the *entire* story, story by story.

AMEN.

Searching for Free
and Responsible

L OVE.

Like a Greek tragedy, which reveals the end at the beginning, we just began this sermon with the last word: *love.*

As we begin this morning, a brief preface: practicing a vibrant Unitarian Universalism is a creative and dynamic act.

Like an artist with a grand vision, we UUs often need to embrace the idea of negative capability and keep uncertainties, mysteries, doubts swirling in our heads and hearts.

I also want to be as blunt as a concrete block on a specific point that will likely upset fundamentalists on both sides of the free speech versus antiracism issue roiling this denomination generally, and this congregation specifically: systems of oppression need to be defined, recognized, and dismantled within society at large, and one of the most effective tools to accomplish this long overdue goal is to fiercely engage in free speech and free inquiry.

These two projects are not independent of each other, and they are not mutually exclusive.

A vibrant and dynamic Unitarian Universalism calls us to responsibly do both, to create a just and equitable world for everyone while encouraging people to freely think and feel and explore, with a robust responsibility.

Key concept, responsibility.

I also want to recognize that responsible and loving engagement in a congregational setting can require self-editing, self-control, and simple good manners. Think of it this way: If your vegan neighbor is coming over for dinner, it is bad form to serve them steak tartar, raw oysters, and barbecued chicken. You are, of course, *free* to serve three delicious meat courses representing the fleshy bounty of land, air, and sea, though you risk being seen as unneighborly, if not downright mean.

Also, just for the record, shelved in my personal library are three books that I know better than to lobby to be part of the circulating library at church: *The Anarchist Cookbook*, *Practical LSD Manufacture*, and the "two books in one" mass market paperback *The Official Black Folks/White Folks Joke Book*.

To me these are interesting texts, and they are part of my personal First Amendment library. I checked a few days ago, and you too can acquire all three books in an online shopping spree for about forty bucks plus shipping.

We should all be very proud that we live in a country where an individual can—if they so choose—purchase these books, read them, shelve them, and not be freaked out that the books will put anyone at risk of arrest. Just as I would never knowingly serve raw oysters to a vegan, I would never advocate that these publications become central texts in a religious context, but I do fiercely defend their availability in a secular context.

And speaking of secular context: Among the countless words written and published, whispered and chanted, yodeled and sung over the course of human history, and among the shredded papers, deleted files, bonfires fueled by banned books, and censorship both active and passive, here are twenty words—in English—for your consideration, "Language is courage: the ability to conceive a thought, to speak it, and by doing so to make it true."

Those words were composed by a writer of great imagination and courage, and as we enter a discussion entitled "Searching for Free and Responsible," we would do well to listen once again to Salman Rushdie, a sentence from his novel *The Satanic Verses*: "Language is courage: the ability to conceive a thought, to speak it, and by doing so to make it true."

[   ]

Do you hear that?

That *silence* is what some religious and political fundamentalists have been trying to do to Salman Rushdie for decades. Indeed, Rushdie was brutally attacked at Chautauqua Institution—a legendary retreat center that practices deep inquiry and free thinking—on the stage in a space called the Hall of Philosophy. And so we speak aloud Rushdie's words, "Language is courage," inside this room called "sanctuary."

"Philosophy" means love of knowledge and wisdom. "Sanctuary" is the most sacred part of a religious building and a place of refuge and protection.

The lecture Rushdie was about to deliver was on the theme "More Than Shelter," and according to local press accounts, the topics to be discussed included "the United States as a place for asylum for writers and other artists in exile and as a home for freedom of creative expression."

This pulpit, three thousand miles from Chautauqua Institution, in a small town near the edge of a continent, is called a "free pulpit." This congregation courageously grants, to whoever speaks from this pulpit, freedom to say what they will, to speak their truth. To think and feel and articulate what they will. To give voice to ideas that may crack your heart open, that may enliven your spirit, that may stir forgotten, perhaps painful memories or inspire you to consider difficult or beautiful or confounding ideas.

At this very moment, each person present here is co-creating a living, breathing, vibrant sanctuary where freedom of thought and freedom of expression is called forth, and I want to assure you that I respect your creation and will do my best to responsibly honor your trust.

And I wonder aloud whether anyone at Chautauqua Institution was instructed to remove the bloodstains of a great writer off the wooden stage in the Hall of Philosophy.

Whether someone with a galvanized bucket of warm water and a scrub brush worked up a lather, and the soapy water turned from sudsy white to murky pink, or whether, upon deeper consideration, the leadership allowed Rushdie's blood to seep deeply in, to stain the floorboards. To keep this stain, this random shape, as a testament and reminder.

If it were my choice, I would keep the stain.

I would invite the world's finest photographers to record the stain in a variety of lights and angles, to publish the images of the stain on the internet for all to see, and to print posters and postcards and T-shirts to send to every library, every house of worship, every statehouse and school and city hall, and the caption would read "Language is courage: the ability to conceive a thought, to speak it, and by doing so to make it true."

Starting here, at this free pulpit co-created in a room called sanctuary, we human beings—whose hearts are pumping our own warm blood—have much work to do in this world, and much work to do within our denomination.

For those of you who are new to UU—or for those who need a quick briefing—Unitarian Universalism is a liberal religion that is, by design, creedless. At its most basic, the word "creedless" simply means that nobody involved in this religion—at any level—will hand you a list of precepts and say, "Here. This is the creed. If you want to be part of our 'we,' you need to believe in and act upon these words."

That said, in Unitarian Universalism, we do share seven principles that frame the structure of the religion and provide guidance for our behavior in the world. The seven principles are not the words of a divine creator, like the Koran of Islam or the Ten Commandments of the Hebrew scriptures; they were not spoken by a messiah and recorded by disciples like the Christian Gospels; they are not like the discourses of the Buddha, nor are they "sacred" in a traditional religious sense.

The seven principles are good ideas—good, working ideas—composed and constructed and enacted by human beings. These ideas are made of words, they are made of language. These ideas did not exist before human beings imagined the ideas, and within cosmic time—as our sun moves toward dying and evaporating the water on our gorgeous blue planet—the seven principles of Unitarian Universalism will also evaporate, because there will be no more human beings to think and imagine them.

Sometimes in our sanctuaries we sound like French Existential-ists, *n'est pas?*

So take heart. Currently, between the nothing of "before human consciousness and imagination were around" and the nothing of "a billion years from now our sun will boil off the planet's oceans and roast everything that's left," we have each other, meeting in this sanctuary, affirming and promoting and calling into being seven principles of a liberal religion.

We are the religion. *We* put the religion into motion and make it manifest in the world. This is a good way to spend a portion of your life's energy and to help build a just and joyous society.

The lack of divine authorship for the seven principles of Unitar-ian Universalism is in no way a diminishment of the principles. Quite the opposite, in fact. Like the Bach cello suites or the Tacoma Narrows Bridge, a cultivated garden or a skillfully con-structed quilt, the principles are made things. Made by human beings. And they are made to be functional and beautiful; they are made to work and nourish and inspire human engagement in a complicated and complex human society, which seems to become more complicated and more complex with every passing news cycle.

The seven principles are also made to work together. The prin-ciples come as a package deal, and their strength lies within the interplay amongst and between, in the push and the pull, in any creative tensions that may arise. In other words, it's fudging a bit if you cherry-pick one or two principles and ignore the others. If you find yourself dismissing or ignoring a certain principle, it would be a constructive and nutritious exercise to explore why you feel no love for this one or that one.

And while the principles exist as an interworking and intercon-nected set of seven, it is also a helpful exercise to occasionally meditate on single principles, to try to understand what the words are actually saying. What you believe the words to mean. How you bring the principles to life.

Not to play favorites, but one of my go-to principles is number four.

Sure, the first principle is the marquee principle that sets everything up—"the inherent worthiness and dignity of every person." This idea is a gorgeous and necessary reminder that even the person who cut you off in traffic or the internet troll who stole your identity is a sublime miracle made of stardust, and that they, too, are a fellow human being pumping warm blood, who contains worthiness and dignity.

That said, it doesn't take too much imagination to get uncomfortable with the first principle, to plop it down in front of an extreme example to see how well it holds up. More than once, after a sermon discussing the first principle, congregants have come up to me and said, "Really?" Then they rattle off a short list of evildoers and ask, with an edge to their voice, "What about *these* guys?"

Or after today's sermon, it is fair to ask, "What about the young man who shoved a sharp blade into Salman Rushdie's neck in front of an audience in a place called the Hall of Philosophy? Show me the worthiness. Show me the dignity. Even his mother has disavowed him."

Not infrequently, worthiness and dignity can be difficult to detect, especially in the extreme. I get it. And yet, speaking for myself, I function better in the world when I believe that human consciousness has worthiness and dignity, that all human beings are worthy of respect, and that an individual's human consciousness is rare and holy and precious and temporal. And also that there are people who enact evil, who misuse and abuse their precious gift, that there are powerful forces within society—racism, fundamentalist capitalism, and fundamentalist religion, to name three—that can blur or bury or blunt an individual's or a group's worthiness and dignity.

As I have implied, human society is a constructed thing. We make it up. As such, we are responsible for helping to maintain and improve it. Difficult as it can be to defend in the extreme, I choose to believe, as a default setting, that every person's consciousness is divine, is rare, and part of my religious practice is to recognize the divine in every person—especially when it's not obvious.

I hate to break it to you, but religion may be best practiced when and where the world does not make sense.

And then of course, the concluding principle, number seven, calls us to have "respect for the interdependent web of all existence"—aka the entirety of the known Universe—"of which we are a part." Note that the operative word is "interdependent," not "interconnected." The difference is worthy of deep consideration.

Between those two poles—from each and every inherently worthy person of principle one to the interdependent web of all existence in principle seven, we find number four, the middle principle. Consider the structure that literally makes "search" the bull's-eye: three principles before, three principles after, and then the word "search" is the exact middle word in a nine-word sentence—four words before, four words after. Whether this is random or not, whether it is intentional or not, the word "search" is the absolute center of our seven principles, the middle point or fulcrum between teeter and totter, between the individual human and the interdependent web of all existence.

It is a very short word, a single syllable—"search"—that serves as both a noun and a verb.

I search my search.
You search your search.
We search our search.

And what is the goal of my, your, and our search? The principle states it plainly: truth and meaning. How shall we search? Once again, the principle makes it plain: freely and responsibly.

I hate to break it to you, but practicing Unitarian Universalism ain't that easy.

Again, Unitarian Universalism offers no sacred texts authored by a divine being. There are no easy outs by saying, "I guess it's God's will." All we have is each other, and our brains and hearts and hands, and our integrity and best intentions. Our love for each other. And, of course, our search.

As Reverend Paige Getty says in the book *The Seven Principles in Word and Worship,* "As a faith tradition, Unitarian Universalism makes sacred the right and responsibility to engage in [a] free and responsible quest as an act of religious devotion. Institutionally, we have left open the questions of what truth and meaning are, acknowledging that mindful people will, in every age, discover new insights."

I love that she describes the search as an "act of religious devotion" and reminds us that "mindful people will, in every age, discover new insights."

True to those words, please be aware that our denomination is currently engaged in a dynamic and comprehensive review of these seven principles, to see whether and how to modify them as our religion moves forward into the twenty-first century. This intentional review is baked into our bylaws, and I invite you to recognize and welcome the process as a part of a "free and responsible search for truth and meaning."

The Unitarian Universalist Association website states,

> Unitarian Universalism is a living tradition that learns and adapts to meet the needs of each generation . . . The digital age has shifted our interactions with community and truth. The COVID-19 pandemic has highlighted our interdependence, and where individualism falls short. There is a rise in global autocracies and attacks on democratic institutions, and climate catastrophe and mass extinctions threaten the delicate balance of the web of life. These are just a few of the major struggles our living tradition must face today and in our future. With the articulation of our shared UU values, we can be better equipped to make values-based decisions in facing these new and evolving realities.

Potent phrase, "new and evolving realities."

Truth be told, we humans have always been searching for truth and meaning and insight within "new and evolving realities."

Twenty-five hundred years ago, Socrates was hanging out in Athens, eager to dialogue with just about anyone about truth and meaning, love, justice, friendship, state power, virtue, et cetera. Topics that can be simultaneously crystal clear and murky. Ideas that can have radically varied expressions and understandings in different cultures.

As you likely know, Socrates was considered the wisest of all human beings for one simple reason: he kept asking questions. As he says in the dialogue entitled "The Apology," "If I am the wisest man alive, it is for I know one thing, and that is that I know nothing." He *knew* that he didn't know.

What I hear in that Socratic sentence, from one of the intellectual wellsprings of Western society, is "search." And thus Socrates tried to find someone wiser than he—that was his search—and would discuss with anyone who cared to try to articulate, through human language, the essence of deeply held human concerns such as justice and love and friendship and power.

We're still talking about these subjects.

And in Socrates's case, his search led to his execution by the state, on charges of impiety and corrupting the youth. Beware: searching and seeking and philosophizing can be as dangerous as it is fulfilling.

With Socrates in mind, with Salman Rushdie without the use of an eye or a hand, and with Rushdie's attacker presumed innocent until proven guilty, we close with a quote from the president of Chautauqua Institution, who addressed the media soon after the attack: "We also saw something else today that I hope we never forget. We saw some of the best of humanity . . . people who ran *toward* danger. I saw Chautauquans who are doctors and nurses rush to provide selfless care, literally holding Salman Rushdie together until the ambulance arrived."

May we all, when called, become the best of humanity.

We certainly practiced this morning, by actively co-creating a free pulpit and co-creating a place called sanctuary. Let's savor our sweet good fortune that our free and responsible search brought us right here, right now. And that our search—the absolute center of this faith tradition—continues responsibly, continues freely—with a fierce drive toward justice fueled by a generous and joyous love.

AMEN.

DOWNSIZING TO YOUR
CABIN(ET) OF WONDERS

Y OU'VE all heard the word "downsize," and you've likely engaged in the process in one form or another.

In our county and culture, the acquisition and management of physical objects is a large part of how we spend our time. In fact, our consumer economy is based on a perpetual cycle of acquisition and consumption. And if our economy is to grow, then consumption necessarily needs to grow as well—whether more people buy stuff or the same people buy more stuff. And more stuff. And *more* stuff . . .

Some economists consider this model a malady and call it "affluenza," and affluenza leads to a very uncomfortable, possibly spiritually deadening state called "stuffocation."

And with stuffocation in mind, I stand before you with polar opposite influences as my constant companions, one on each shoulder. I have a naturalist on one side and an artist on the other. Each one whispers in an ear; each one blesses me with strong and compelling influences.

On this shoulder, with a memoir of his life at Walden Pond, the great nineteenth-century individualist and naturalist, walker and journal writer, tax protester and civil disobedience icon, Henry David Thoreau.

And on this shoulder, with his surrealist assemblage boxes constructed from objects and images gathered from junk shops and used bookstores, the reclusive collector and Christian Scientist who lived with his mother in Queens, New York, Joseph Cornell.

Henry David Thoreau and Joseph Cornell, I love you both.

We all have some swirl of competing influences within us— gracefully and universally symbolized by the yin–yang symbol of Taoism. The staying power of this yin–yang symbol lies in the fact that opposites not only coexist but also create a coherent and striking whole, and that the opposites necessarily exist within the other—that small circle of black within the white, the white within the black—and that there is not one without the other. The interlocking curves and embedded circles create movement, dynamism, relationship, tension, and a deep honoring of the other.

And so my intention today is to enter the yin–yang world of urban collector Joseph Cornell and rural minimalist Henry David Thoreau, to explore relationships with the material world and to discover essential things to house in our cabins and/or display in our cabinets of wonder.

As Unitarians, we all know of Henry David Thoreau. And frankly we would love nothing more than to claim him as one of our own. And while there is a UU fellowship named after Thoreau, and his mentor and friend Ralph Waldo Emerson was a Unitarian minister, Thoreau was not a joiner and never became a member of a fellowship.

That said, he did write *Walden*, one of the essential books of the American canon, and it is certainly on the short list of source materials for Unitarians, especially regarding our seventh principle, "the interdependent web of all existence."

It is quite likely that you have some sort of relationship with *Walden*—from hating reading the turgid text in eighth grade to taking the "Walden pond" metaphor deep into your life, or perhaps you decided to downsize your life to essentials after reading this quote: "Simplicity, simplicity, simplicity! I say, let your affairs be as two or three, and not a hundred or a thousand; instead of a million count half a dozen, and keep your accounts on your thumb nail."

Thoreau is the patron saint of downsizing. In the first chapter of *Walden*, he enumerates his list of bare necessities: food, shelter, clothing, fuel.

From this spare list of absolute needs, he moved carefully to enumerate a few more objects essential to his life. Early in *Walden*, he writes, "At the present day, and in this country, as I find by my own experience, a few implements, a knife, an axe, a spade, a wheelbarrow, etc., and for the studious, lamplight, stationery, and access to a few books, rank next to necessaries, and can all be obtained for a trifling cost."

"Cost" is a key word here. Thoreau is trying to determine the minimum amount of life energy he needs to invest to acquire those necessaries that keep body and soul together. He knows that if he wants something beyond the essentials, he pays some of his life, in the form of work—which takes time—to acquire and maintain it.

What Thoreau wants most is time. *Life-time.*

Assuming that the essentials are taken care of, what then? Thoreau illustrates this precisely in the first chapter of *Walden:* "I had three pieces of limestone on my desk, but I was terrified to find that they required to be dusted daily, when the furniture of my mind was all undusted still, and I threw them out the window in disgust."

Thoreau, in essence, is the ultimate downsizer. During his experiment at Walden Pond, he reduced things to the bare essentials and then reintroduced things quite deliberately, with deep and nuanced consideration.

We can imagine his cabin looking very spare, and everything in it present for a reason.

I confess to you that my house does not look like this. I also confess that I have a secret dream that it would. Imagine being in a space with nothing superfluous, with everything at hand useful and purposeful.

As a person enamored with objects, it might seem odd that I have such an affinity for Thoreau's ideals. In fact, when a member of our congregation heard I was delivering a sermon on downsizing, her response was something like "Oh, he's one to talk!"

It's true. I have a natural affinity for collecting things, for organizing and categorizing and storing, for objects of interest and beauty, for art. As a person enamored with objects, I brush Thoreau from my shoulder when I walk into thrift stores and estate sales and library sales and indulge myself with little treats, like books with wacky titles or covers, such as:

Health by Stunts

Applied Mathematics for Girls

How to Be Happy Though Married

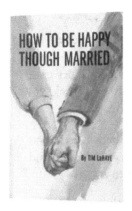  

I have been collecting things since I was a kid, and when I approached my most recent birthday, I found Thoreau on my shoulder, whispering into my ear that I should "get my affairs in order."

I was that guy with a wife, two kids, a cat, a car, a house, and too much stuff, including two unicycles I couldn't even ride.

Very un-Thoreauvian.

I felt compelled to downsize, to minimize, to clear my mind and life of useless clutter, to take a necessary step toward essential things.

Did you ever hear the phrase "When the student is ready, the teacher will appear"? Just when I began "getting my affairs in order," I got a call from an artist whose work I deeply admire. He invited me to his studio for a piece of artwork, because he was moving and he didn't want to take it all with him.

While this seems a bit counterintuitive during a fit of downsizing, I went to Robert's studio and was ecstatic.

I love his work—his painting, his sculptures, his sketches, his mind—*everything*. I was sad to hear that he was moving away, across the country to New England, within a day's drive of Walden Pond. He and his wife were taking only one truckload of things. A small truck. So decisions had to be made.

As it is Robert's practice to be precise and deliberate, here was his process: he was touching every physical object in his life and making a decision: "Do I carry this with me into Act 3?"

That's what he called his sixties and beyond, Act 3.

This is very much like Thoreau's own project—trying to determine essential things.

Robert had *just* turned sixty. He was downsizing and moving in one fell swoop, and I got to help the process by being gifted a piece of art. I also *bought* a piece of art. "To pay for the gas to get across Nebraska," I told him.

And he claimed that what he didn't sell or give away he was going to recycle. I thought about renting a storage unit and becoming his recycle bin, but I honored his process and, to use a favorite word, his flow.

To provide a bit more context, let us go back in time, five years before standing in this artist's studio. I was on a business trip in New York City and visited the legendary Strand Bookstore. This is a vast and deep and incredible place for books, and their slogan is "Where books find you." And it was there that a book about the artist Joseph Cornell found me.

Cornell, I discovered, was a lifelong bachelor who lived with his mother and a brother with cerebral palsy. He would commute by train into Manhattan and haunt used bookstores and junk shops, searching for interesting images and objects to incorporate into his art. His basement was his workshop and storage area, floor-to-ceiling shelves jumbled with files and boxes labeled "seashells" and "balls" and "glasses" and "cutout birds."

Cornell described the contents of his files as, "A diary journal repository laboratory, picture gallery, museum, sanctuary, observatory, key . . . the core of labyrinth, a clearinghouse for dreams and visions . . . childhood regained."

It would likely drive Thoreau around the bend—the urban setting, the stuffed house, the basement so far from open air, the overbearing mother.

But in the night, when Cornell's house was quiet, he would go to the basement, to the workshop, and take objects from his inventory and images from his files and place them inside wooden boxes, in relationship to each other. Relationships to make art.

And when the elements were just so, when they were in proper relationship, he would front the box with glass to make a little "cabinet of wonder."

With my book on Joseph Cornell, the cross-country flight went by in a snap. I spent hours looking at Cornell's boxes. My world was getting that much larger, that much deeper.

To get home from the airport—a hundred-mile trip—I took a train to a passenger ferry and then planned to take two buses the last fifty miles. The bus schedules and connections were less than ideal, so those last fifty miles would have taken hours.

Just as I was steeling myself for the last two legs of a long journey, I recognized one of the ferry passengers. The hitchhiker in me decided to ask this familiar person whether he was heading back to town, and if so, would he be willing to give me a ride. He agreed.

I knew that he was an artist and I had attended one of his gallery exhibitions. As we settled into the car ride, I said, "Can I ask you about an artist I just discovered?"

"Sure," Robert said.

"Do you know anything about Joseph Cornell?"

There was a long pause, and then Robert looked at me. "*Major influence*," he said.

We spent the entire ride talking excitedly about Cornell. I was on the front end of discovery, and Robert shared stories of his long relationship with the work.

At the time, there was an art exhibit in our town that featured boxes that were very Cornellesque. The pieces were compelling, but they did not affect me as powerfully as the photographs in this book about Cornell, so I asked Robert, "What makes Cornell Cornell?"

And the answer I got is exactly why I love talking with poets and artists.

"Joseph Cornell became the bird."

By this, Robert meant that in the act of his creation, Cornell moved beyond making an assemblage that was simply beautiful or visually stunning—he experienced freedom in making assemblages. He shape-shifted right out of his circumstance of living with his mother in Queens and entered into other worlds altogether. He transformed castaway objects from the vast jumble of objects and created art.

"Joseph Cornell became the bird."

Now we jump forward from the flashback, into Robert's studio. I am gifted a gorgeous sculpture and also buy another, and we make a date for coffee so I can talk with Robert about his project of downsizing, of touching everything he owns and making a decision about what comes along for that cross-country ride into Act 3.

It turns out that the project took much longer than Robert expected, not only because there were a lot of objects but also because many of the objects had power, what some people call "mojo." For example, he found an old college notebook from a class with a famous writer—he did not get along well with the writer, and in reading his notebooks, Robert realized he had never "finished" the class.

There was a concentrated knot of psychic energy around this notebook, and he realized that while physically discarding the notebook was expedient, he was being called to truly finish the class, to now learn the lesson that the class had offered, to finally move beyond this teacher, who, for him, was a psychic sandbag. To allow *flow*.

And that was a lesson for me. This practice of getting one's affairs in order was more than carting a few boxes of discards to the thrift store or the dumpster. The deeper you go, the more mojo you may discover. And you may have to move some sandbags.

We all know objects can hold power: The chew toy from a dead dog. That heirloom bowl Grandma Mae brought over from Bohemia. A dirty pot holder your kid weaved in kindergarten.

And as we downsize, let's be fascinated by what we keep and what we release.

The famous literary critic Harold Bloom says the reason we have a literary canon is because we die. If we could live forever, we could read everything. Because we die, we need to make choices about what is worthy to read, how we want to invest our reading time.

This statement is about the limits of personal time and the lasting value of brilliant literature.

There are also the limits of space. Thoreau's cabin was only so big. He had a small desk—enough to hold some papers and a pencil, and to give him a world of room to write.

Cornell's cabinets are also small, and yet they, too, contain worlds. In his book *Dime-Store Alchemy: The Art of Joseph Cornell*, Charles Simic reminds us that "It ought to be clear that Cornell is a religious artist. Vision is his subject. He makes holy icons."

I like that the words "cabin" and "cabinet" are related, and here is a little fantasy. If I could time travel, I'd go back to Queens, New York, in the 1940s or '50s and buy one of Cornell's boxes—his holy icons—then time travel back another century to Walden Pond. When Thoreau left for his daily walk, I'd slip into his cabin and hang Cornell's box above Thoreau's desk. My selection would be one of Cornell's famous bird boxes, *Great Horned Owl with Harvest Moon*.

Of course I'd spy on Thoreau when he returned, to watch him respond to this miraculous gift.

Let's imagine Thoreau—that fierce downsizer—discovering the piece, standing before it, and gazing in. He leans in to get a closer look, and when the sun goes down, he watches this moon-dense cabinet by candlelight. He even hears an owl hooting, and wonders about the source.

In the cool, rational light of morning, Thoreau would come to that piece of mysterious Art intent on taking it down and moving it out, to join those three pieces of limestone we talked about earlier. He reaches up, then pauses. Once again he's seduced by the mystery of this piece.

He reaches up, and rather than remove the box from the wall, he wipes the dust from the top edge.

Imagine Thoreau finding that first *something* he is willing to dust. Of course that first something would be Art—mysterious and compelling and unexplainable Art that enriched his life.

And after dusting, let's then imagine he sat at his desk and was inspired to write this sentence from *Walden:* "Before we can adorn our houses with beautiful objects the walls must be stripped, and beautiful housekeeping and beautiful living be laid for a foundation."

I ask us all: Have we sufficiently stripped the walls of our houses? And once we have, what shall we allow inside our cabinets and inside our cabins?

When we practice downsizing, what remains and why? Because what remains, and how we place it in relationship, says much about who we are—what we care for, what we work for, what we value.

This is where you are called to become the artist—the artist of your own life and living areas. You are not only cleaning out your closets; you are composing the space within which your life will flourish.

In downsizing, let's find that limestone and those sandbags in our lives—objects we shouldn't be wasting our time dusting and lugging—and rid ourselves of them.

And yet . . .

I arrive at that point and long for Cornell's basement, those boxes and files, a curated jumble of flotsam and jetsam—the raw materials for cabinets of wonder.

So there it is, the yin and the yang: Thoreau's walls atop Cornell's basement, the walls stripped bare and the basement, that "core of labyrinth," teeming. And when, from the basement, there comes a cabinet of wonder to be placed on the wall, we marvel. When we reach to dust this holy icon, when we care for that Art, let our arms become wings and the dust rag feathers.

Let us *all* become the bird.

AMEN.

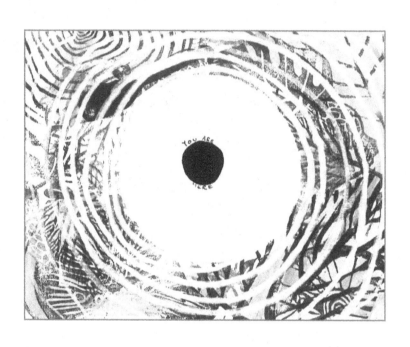

POSTCARDS FROM
YOUR SPIRITUAL JOURNEY

THIS SPRING I shared a conversation with an elderly gentleman who is preparing to celebrate his ninetieth birthday. Part of his preparation is to downsize, to rid himself of physical stuff. While discussing his deliberate process of how he is moving things out of his life, he said this gorgeous sentence: "I want to write my spiritual journey."

How glorious, I thought, and I wondered whether the release of physical objects provided the necessary mental space and creative drive for him to consider spiritual matters. Instead of inheriting a teapot made by a famous potter or a first edition of *Winnie-the-Pooh*, I'm certain that his family would much rather have a memoir of his spiritual journey, written in his own words.

And in reflecting on that ambitious statement, "I want to write my spiritual journey," I came to realize that our individual and specific and idiosyncratic spiritual journey may be the deepest realm of our autobiography, of our lived experience on this planet.

"What is one of your stories?" I asked. "Imagine writing me a postcard from along The Way."

"Well," he said . . .

I recently presented a talk to a congregation wherein I employed two foundational concepts from classical mathematics to help illustrate some broader points about religion. The concepts mentioned were the simple fact that parallel lines never meet, and the transitive property of equality, which states that if A = B and B = C, then A = C. Bedrock math. We played with the idea of metaphorical equal signs and compared the wisdom statements of Buddha, Jesus, and Lao Tzu. For example, here are two wisdom statements that find a home in the Golden Rule file:

Jesus said, "Do to others as you would have them do to you."

Buddha said, "Consider others as yourself."

Sounds like a dreamy Sunday morning, yes?

It is important to note that this story is set at a Unitarian Universalist congregation, and we had just spent twenty minutes interweaving bedrock math and religious wisdom statements. Immediately after the presentation, a retired doctor met me at the pulpit and said, "You're not quite right about that equal sign."

Our good doctor continued, "In quantum mathematics, A doesn't *necessarily* equal C." His eyes were sparkling as I welcomed the feedback and said that I needed to brush up on my quantum mathematics.

Then, at coffee hour, a retired professor told me, "In Euclidian plane geometry, parallel lines never meet. But quantum mechanics suggests that parallel lines *may* meet." Her eyes were sparkling as I welcomed the feedback and said that I needed to brush up on my quantum mechanics.

What the sparkling eyes of the doctor and the sparkling eyes of the professor betrayed is the delight in broadening context and reminding us that what we see with our own eyes and mind may not necessarily reflect ultimate reality.

There are vast universes of thought and experience and imagination that your brain and heart and soul have yet to visit or register or perceive or comprehend. This is an invitation to an exhilarating curiosity and radical humility.

So the word of the day that Sunday morning was "quantum."

True to my word about brushing up on those realms "quantum," after I arrived home from church, I went to my office and pulled down the one book I knew that I owned with the word "quantum" in its title: *The Quantum Bigfoot.*

Yes, Bigfoot. As in Sasquatch.

Since I was a little boy I've had a soft spot in my heart for Bigfoot, and as a mature adult I've gathered together books about Bigfoot. A few years ago, moreover, I attended a lecture by a Bigfoot researcher. To help financially support his ambitious efforts, I bought several of his books and a CD of recorded Bigfoot sounds. And consider this quote from his introduction to *The Quantum Bigfoot*: "In this book I am persuaded to present a reasonable correlation between the rules of quantum science as the foundation of spirituality, and how it could relate to these creatures known as Bigfoot."

Did you catch that? "The rules of quantum science as the foundation of spirituality."

Which brings us to a famous quote by Albert Einstein, who was no stranger to the word "quantum":

> The most beautiful emotion we can experience is the mystical. It is the power of all true art and science. [They] to whom this emotion is a stranger, who can no longer wonder and stand rapt in awe, [are] as good as dead. To know that what is impenetrable to us really exists, manifesting itself as the highest wisdom and the most radiant beauty, which our dull faculties can comprehend only in their most primitive forms—this knowledge, this feeling, is at the center of true religiousness. In this sense, and in this sense only, I belong to the rank of devoutly religious [people].

I love that idea. "The most beautiful emotion we can experience is the mystical. It is the power of all true art and science." I recently witnessed the mystical come to life before my very eyes.

Postcard One

My neighbor, I'll call him Mr. X, was taking his morning walk around the block. Mr. X is an ex-Marine, an ex–psychology teacher, and an ex–back-to-the-lander. He's tough as nails, drinks strong Negronis every evening, rides a bicycle, loves to kayak, soaks most days in his hot tub, plays the banjo and guitar, and is a devout atheist who teases me about attending church.

"Hey Mr. X," I said, when I saw him, "how's it going?"

He stopped walking and looked in my direction. "Everything is so *beautiful*," he said.

This did not sound like Mr. X. Please know, it was an average winter morning on the Olympic Peninsula: sun behind clouds, misty gray, cool temperature.

"What's beautiful?" I asked as I crossed the street to be near him.

"Everything! *Everything!* I'm just overwhelmed by it all. Look at that branch. It's so beautiful!"

With his cane he pointed to a leafless cherry tree, which in a few months will be festooned with blossoms and then, with the help of pollinators, delicious red cherries.

I could see Mr. X's eyes were brimming with tears and I instinctively knew I was in the presence of a human being having a profound experience, what I will call a "spiritual experience." We were not atop the Himalayas or practicing yoga in an ashram or walking the labyrinth in Chartres Cathedral. We were neighbors standing side by side along the weedy edge of the road, on an early morning in January, with gray mist in the air, admiring the beauty of a bare branch of a cherry tree.

And an old man's eyes were filling with tears because the world was so utterly, fabulously, profoundly beautiful.

I chose to be silent, to not respond with words. To simply be with my neighbor, to bear witness to what was happening, and nod at the words he was inspired to share: "Just look at that branch!"

I could have been in the presence of William Blake or Teresa of Ávila or Rumi. The branch *was* beautiful, though truth be told, I was looking with my eyes while Mr. X was seeing with his entire being. *Seeing* the branch with his eyes rimmed with tears.

"The most beautiful emotion we can experience is the mystical. It is the power of all true art and science."

Postcard Two

This past fall, a young person I know was hospitalized for ten days with a manic episode. They had never experienced mania, and while in the hospital they experienced a psychotic break. Eventually they were diagnosed with bipolar disorder type 1.

"Classic case," said the psychiatrist.

This is all new territory for them.

After being released from the hospital, I had the opportunity to spend a day with this person and listen to their stories about how they are trying to figure out what happened, how to stay grounded, how to manage the regimes of medicine and therapy, and what lies ahead.

They also shared that their mania was a profound experience, what they called a spiritual experience. Other people in their life, those helping them through their hospitalization—doctors, nurses, loved ones—always called the phenomenon "mania," a symptom of mental illness. But this person bristles at the phrase "mental illness," though they never want to return to the depression that preceded the mania, during which they suffered—for the first time in their life—suicidal ideation.

"In the hospital, my favorite therapy sessions were called 'music therapy,' where we would just listen to music," they said. "When I got out of the hospital I was listening to music and this song came up on my feed. A song I had never heard, by an artist I didn't know, but after the last note faded I pressed Play on my phone and listened again. And then again. And again. I just loved this song. Do you want to hear it?"

"Definitely! I *definitely* want to hear that song," I said.

They beseeched the internet gods to send the song through their phone by pressing Play—the best button on the planet, by the way, Play—and sound filled the air. Vaguely familiar guitar, and then the lyrics started and I instantly recognized the words. This was a deep-cut song by an independent folk singer, and the opening lyrics go like this:

> Inside the tunnels, the stone tunnels, are the trains,
> And inside the trains, the steel trains, are the bags of skin,
> And inside the thin skin are the blood and the bones,
> And inside the blood and the bones are the dreams.
> It really is that simple. It really is that fragile.

> I am one such dream inside the blood and the bags and the bones and the trains and the tunnels.
> There's a dream sitting next to me
> And there's a dream across from me,
> Fragile . . .

"I *love* that song," I said. "I once saw this very same folk singer live at a very small venue, and after the show I bought a stack of his CDs. On a recent road trip, I grabbed one of the discs—a random choice—and listened to it while driving down Highway 101.

"After I heard that song you just played," I said, "I pressed Play, over and over. I probably listened to the song ten or twelve times in a row, just like you were doing, three thousand miles away. Given the timing, we might have been pressing Play at the very same moment."

Pause. How weird and coincidental and quantum is that?

The song is called "The Dreams," by Peter Mulvey, and it ends with these lyrics:

> We all know that one day
> The tunnels will crumble and the trains will stop
> And the blood and the bags and the bones will be gone,
> And in between now and then we know something must
>   happen to every dream.
> I don't know what will happen to the other dreams
> But I know what will happen to me,
> Sure as rain, I know,
> Sure as winter:
> I'll breathe and grieve and struggle and strive and love,
>   love, and love,
> And if I'm lucky, once, just once, the dream will drop to
>   the floor like a vase and shatter in shards of silence,
> But I will see, I will see in the pattern of the pieces, I will
>   see . . .
> Something.
>
> This will, this will, this will happen.
> But now the train with all its precious cargo
> Rolls on.

One aspect of what my friend loved about the song was the line "I will see, I will see in the pattern of the pieces, I will see . . . Something."

Because in their mania they saw patterns everywhere, they were able to make connections where there were—formerly—no discernible connections to make. A classic symptom of mania, this making of connections. And perhaps it is in a manic state when the seventh principle of Unitarian Universalism reveals itself most vividly: "Respect for the interdependent web of all existence of which we are a part."

Again, Einstein: "The most beautiful emotion we can experience is the mystical. It is the power of all true art and science."

Postcard Three

Your postcard. A story from your spiritual journey.

Perhaps you are like the millions of people with addictions to drugs or alcohol who entered treatment and began working the Twelve Steps. If you are sober and clean, you can likely tell us a vivid story of a spiritual experience along your journey toward sobriety, a spiritual journey if ever there was one.

Perhaps you took LSD at a Grateful Dead show and danced like a whirling dervish and became the heartbeat of the Universe.

Perhaps you sat in meditation and experienced that initial awakening called *kenshō*.

Perhaps the world opened up at the birth of your child.

Perhaps the world opened up at the death of your spouse.

I knew an attorney from Los Angeles who was victim of a violent assault and who, after emerging from a coma, gave up his law practice, changed his name, and traveled to India searching for deeper meanings. Decades later, his memorial service was standing room only, and the love expressed by those in mourning was profound.

Perhaps you dove into a cold river after soaking in a hot spring and felt overdrive alive.

Perhaps this morning you sipped tea and truly tasted tea.

Perhaps, perhaps, perhaps . . . the possibilities are endless.

To quote French philosopher and Jesuit priest Pierre Teilhard de Chardin: "We are not human beings having a spiritual experience. We are spiritual beings having a human experience."

Just *look* at that branch!

AMEN.

THANKS AND GRATITUDE

My appreciation to those UU congregations in the Salish Sea region that have invited me to speak. I loved each and every Sunday morning.

A deep bow to my dear friend Dan Gerber. I've been reading Dan's poems for decades and frequently integrate his wise and beautiful words into services, such as:

> I think of my father
> telling me an hour
> before he died,
> how he thought of all the
> men and women he'd loved
> and how
> he wished he'd told them
> when he could've.

A shout-out to Brian Doyle and his exuberant *A Book of Uncommon Prayer*, a volume I have donated to a dozen church libraries. We need more uncommon prayer.

Thanks to Conner Bouchard-Roberts, improvisational and indefatigable publisher of Winter texts, for his guidance and good cheer while bringing this book into being. Conner sports one of the most recognizable laughs in publishing, and any day is brightened by his presence.

Finally, deep appreciation to Todd Manza for his companionship during our years of Wednesday walks, where many of these topics and stories, ideas and images were first bandied about. Manza does not suffer fools gladly, though for some reason (known only to him) he continues to walk with me.

LINER NOTES

They Saw Two Heads

When I first delivered this talk, I used the word "hermaphrodite," and afterwards a person in their twenties informed me that this word is outdated and offensive. I did some research and discovered the preferred term is "intersex" and so made the change. Also, early in this piece I use the phrase "chromosome abnormality" in reference to the condition known as Down syndrome. Using the word "abnormality" seemed at odds with the overall message, but I decided to keep the word after consulting the *Disability Language Style Guide*, published by the National Center on Disability and Journalism. All this to say: language is fluid, culture shifts, and I bow to those who attempt to keep us all current on preferred usage.

How Quiet Silence: [   ]

My thanks to Terry Tempest Williams for the inspiration for this piece. Terry is an amazing presence and a spiritual force. She once texted me a photo of a massive wildfire in Utah and compared the enflamed horizon and night sky to a Mark Rothko painting—*that* is penetrating and creative vision. Thanks also to the Women in Black who stood in silence on Monday mornings on Water Street in Port Townsend. As I accepted the leaflet that was offered, it was powerful to realize that other Women in Black were standing in silence in cities and towns throughout the world. And a deep bow of gratitude to pianist Ikue Goldstein, who played John Cage's *4' 33"* with passion, precision, and understated flair.

Books, articles, and websites consulted for this talk include:

"'A Room of Quiet': The Meditation Room, United Nations Headquarters," www.un.org/Depts/dhl/dag/meditationroom. htm.

One Square Inch of Silence: One Man's Quest to Preserve Quiet, by Gordon Hempton (Atria, 2010).

The Rest Is Noise: Listening to the Twentieth Century, by Alex Ross (Picador, 2007).

"Silence! Why John Cage's *4´33˝* Is No Laughing Matter," by David Stubbs, *The Quietus* website, December 13, 2010.

Talking to My Body, by Anna Swir, translated from Polish by Leonard Nathan and Czesław Miłosz (Copper Canyon Press, 1996).

When Women Were Birds, by Terry Tempest Williams (Crichton Books, 2012).

Figure Out Something

I encourage you to seek out and devour Clemens Starck's *Cathedrals and Parking Lots: Collected Poems* (Empty Bowl, 2019).

When Clem and I presented this talk at my home congregation, Quimper UU Fellowship in Port Townsend, Washington, several of his poet-friends came to listen, including Michael O'Conner, Tim McNulty, Holly Hughes, Red Pine, Finn Wilcox, and Tom Jay. Clem has a lot of friends, and I count myself blessed to be one of them. I love visiting with Clem at his dusty farmhouse in the foothills of the Coast Range in Oregon. There are always stacks of interesting books on the dining room table, cold beer in the fridge, and meaningful conversations during hearty meals. Along with being a poet, Clem is also a film scholar, and one of our rituals during my visits is to retire to the viewing room, sip martinis (very dry, with a twist), and curate mini festivals from the thousands of eccentric DVDs in his film library. We once created a "Films Directed by Hal Ashby" festival that featured a movie I've seen at least fifty times, *Harold and Maude*. Along with being a Unitarian Universalist, I also consider myself a devout Maudeist, and watching *Harold and Maude* with Clem deepened my faith.

Non-uments and Toppled Statues

At the time I presented this talk, American society was convulsing within an environment of polarized politics, media silos, a global COVID-19 pandemic that was killing millions, testy battles between vaxxers and anti-vaxxers, extreme weather brought on by climate change, the murder of Black Americans by white law enforcement officers, the #MeToo movement, the emboldening of right-wing militia groups, an opioid epidemic, increased homelessness, toxic social media, overt attacks on democracy, and chilling manifestations of Orwellian "Ignorance Is Strength" doublethink ideology. It was startling to see bumper stickers reminding us of the obvious: FACTS EXIST. It seemed that every day the phrase "double down" was used to describe the behavior or rhetoric of a person with political power, yet, to my mind, doubling down is an obstacle to understanding and dialogue. Family members and friends whom I love espoused political beliefs and social behaviors I found hard to fathom, and while we attempted to discuss our differences, relationships strained toward breaking.

During this time, Unitarian Universalism was engaged in an uncomfortable and unsettling recognition of and reckoning with white supremacy culture within its own organization—and that reckoning continues. In this talk, which was presented via video conference because of the pandemic, calling forth the layered complexities of Unitarian icon Thomas Jefferson seemed fitting.

Thanks to Annette Gordon-Reed for her impressive and necessary book *Thomas Jefferson and Sally Hemings: An American Controversy* (University of Virginia Press, 1998).

Also, a bow of gratitude to Alberto Ríos's marvelous poem "The Smallest Muscle in the Human Body," from the book of the same name (Copper Canyon Press, 2002).

Searching for Free and Responsible

I grew up on Chautauqua Avenue, in Chautauqua County, near Chautauqua Lake, a few dozen miles from Chautauqua Institution. The attack on Salman Rushdie in the institution's Hall of Philosophy was shocking to my core. I asked my mother to send me clippings from the local newspaper, *The Post-Journal*, and she mailed me the following front-page articles from August 2022:

"Salman Rushdie Attacked Before Giving Chautauqua Address Friday," by staff/wire (August 13)

"Chautauqua President Addresses Future," by Gregory Bacon (August 13)

"Hochul: We Will Stand with Courage," by Michael Zabrodsky (August 15)

Other materials consulted include:

The Seven Principles in Word and Worship, edited by Ellen Brandenburg (Unitarian Universalist Association of Congregations, 2007).

"The Moral Roots of Liberals and Conservatives," by Jonathan Haidt, TED Talk (March 2008).

Downsizing to Your Cabin(et) of Wonders

Robert Reedy was a wonderful visual artist, and he embodied a voracious curiosity that was fed by reading books. Lots and lots of books. I considered it a good day when I saw Robert walking to or from the public library with his backpack stuffed with books. His idea—to touch everything he owned and decide whether to keep the object or release it—predated Marie Kondo's joyful advice in *The Life-Changing Magic of Tidying Up.*

In addition to the papers of Joseph Cornell at the Archives of American Art, Smithsonian Institution, other materials consulted include:

A Convergence of Birds: Original Fiction and Poetry Inspired by the Work of Joseph Cornell, edited by Jonathan Safran Foer (Distributed Art Publishers, 2001).

Joseph Cornell: Navigating the Imagination, edited by Lynda Roscoe Hartigan (Yale University Press, 2007).

"Street-Corner Theology," by Charles Simic, from *Dime-Store Alchemy* (Ecco, 1992).

Walden, by Henry David Thoreau (1854).

Postcards from Your Spiritual Journey

Sasquatch makes an appearance via *The Quantum Bigfoot* (2nd ed.) by Ron Morehead (Sierra Sounds, 2017).

Peter Mulvey is a folk singer par excellence. Please listen to "The Dreams," and consider becoming one of Peter's monthly patrons at petermulvey.com. A writer and storyteller, Peter wrote a fantastic children's book (also very much for adults) called *Vlad the Astrophysicist* (Blooming Twig Books, 2016). There is a TEDx talk available online in which Peter performs *Vlad the Astrophysicist* and uses the sound *pssst* to great effect.

Thanks, also, to my bibliophile friend Chris Faatz, who sends me postcards from his journey.

NOTES ON THE ILLUSTRATIONS

FRONT COVER: The assemblage *Writers Heart* (2015) is by Loran Scruggs. This is one of my favorite pieces of art. Loran took an 18″×24″ piece of 3/4″ plywood, then used tin cans, bottle caps, a brass bowl, golden pens, and brass-coated nails to create a joyful reminder to write to the heart and generate some light. I admire visionaries who can gather discarded scraps and create art, and I enthusiastically encourage you to visit www.loranscruggs.com.

THEY SAW TWO HEADS: Minutes after seeing the pink plus sign on this home pregnancy test, I called work and informed the boss I had to take the day off. He was not pleased; I was delighted.

HOW QUIET SILENCE [   ]: This image is called, appropriately enough, "One Square Inch of Silence." You are welcome to make one of your own from a 3×5 card. You can carry that one square inch of silence in your pocket and place it on anything, anywhere. Works like a charm.

FIGURE OUT SOMETHING: The front cover of a great book of poems. Visit www.emptybowl.org to order a copy.

NON-UMENTS AND TOPPLED STATUES: Based on a vintage medical etching of a human ear. Stapedius is in there somewhere.

SEARCHING FOR FREE AND RESPONSIBLE: When I was a boy, the street signs in Jamestown, New York, changed over to larger reflective signs. This old-school Chautauqua Avenue sign was available for the taking, so I took it. It lives wherever I live.

DOWNSIZING TO YOUR CABIN(ET) OF WONDERS: The owl Henry may have seen inside his cabin, but not before the owl saw Henry.

POSTCARDS FROM YOUR SPIRITUAL JOURNEY: When I told my daughter Opal that I was working on a talk called "Postcards from Your Spiritual Journey," she created this postcard for me. You can look at, watch, and ponder this little image for a long time and keep on seeing things, and the googly eye is seeing you right back.

ABOUT THE AUTHOR

JOSEPH BEDNARIK was raised in Jamestown, New York, grew up in Helsinki, Finland, graduated with a degree in philosophy from Haverford College, and invested his professional career working for nonprofit literary publishers. He has edited and co-edited several books, including *The Sumac Reader* (Michigan State University Press, 1997), *One-Man Boat: The George Hitchcock Reader* (Story Line Press, 2003), and *Jim Harrison: Complete Poems* (Copper Canyon Press, 2022), which was selected as an "Editor's Choice" by *The New York Times Book Review*. Bednarik lives in Port Townsend, Washington, and is a long-time member of Quimper Unitarian Universalist Fellowship.

OVER
ɹǝpun
PUBLISHING

SAVOR YOUR READING TIME.

Printed in the USA
CPSIA information can be obtained
at www.ICGtesting.com
LVHW031224190924
791480LV00004B/140